The Messenger
25992 Portafu
Mission Viejo, CA 92691

W9-BOO-294

OBJECT LESSONS
FOR
YOUTH PROGRAMS

by
H. W. Connelly

BAKER BOOK HOUSE
Grand Rapids, Michigan

Copyright 1964 by
Baker Book House Company

ISBN: 0-8010-2314-9

Fourteenth printing, November 1992

Printed in the United States of America

OBJECT LESSONS FOR YOUTH PROGRAMS

To the hundreds of boys, girls and their leaders
to whom I have told these stories, and who
inspired me to put them in print, I affection-
ately and prayerfully dedicate this volume.

Introduction

It is more than a cliche that our youth are the key to a better day. We have long been concerned that those of experience give more thought to developing the Christian character and witness of our young people.

Out of his long and dedicated ministry, Dr. H. W. Connelly has written this most readable and helpful book.

Those who share his interest in young people will welcome this volume of varied and meaningful suggestions. I would like to commend it especially to pastors, teachers in the Sunday School, and leaders in the Training Union and in other youth groups.

As I have come to know personally the pastors and lay workers of our Virginia Baptist churches, it has been gratifying to learn that many of these have found God's leading for their lives through the guidance and help of Dr. Connelly.

This book is attractively organized and written, with stories of human interest from the author's personal experiences. The suggestions which come from the stories, outlines and materials, cover a variety of practical and stimulating ideas.

In all this Dr. Connelly makes it evident that he never tells a story or makes suggestions without a deep consciousness of the basic needs of the Christian life. Evangelism, missions, stewardship, education, training—these indeed constitute the theme of his book.

Lucius M. Polhill

Foreword

Jesus loves children. He took them in His arms and blessed them and said, "Suffer the little children to come unto me and forbid them not." They loved Jesus. No wonder they placed palm leaves in His path and sang hosannas to Him. Jesus used children in His ministry. He took a little boy's lunch one day and multiplied it and fed more than 5,000 people. He took a little child and set him in the midst and said, "Except ye be converted and become as little children ye shall not enter into the Kingdom." Jesus instituted the Ordinances of Baptism and the Lord's Supper. All of these are, in a sense, Object Lessons. It was His favorite way of getting His truths across to the multitude. See Him pointing to the lily, a net, a coin and the vine. All of these were simple ordinary things that were understood by His audience and with them He illustrated great spiritual truths. We would do well to emulate His example in loving, winning and using children and also teaching them through simple Object Lessons.

In my first pastorate after leaving the seminary, a godly old Presbyterian Minister said to me, "You will make good in the ministry." I replied, "Thank you, why do you think so?" "Because you love children and know how to lead them." My own pastor had talked to me a number of times about the importance of loving and winning children.

I have held over two hundred revival meetings and for a number of years I have used Object Lessons. For about five minutes each service, addressed primarily to the children, I would have them seated near the front, arranged in chairs according to their ages and I noticed that adults would sit on the edge of their seats and lean forward to get the message when I talked to the children. There were more favorable comments about the Object Lessons than about the sermons. When I would return to a community some seven or eight years later, different ones would speak of the Object Lessons I used when there before, rather than telling me about the sermons.

At the first service in a series I would request all boys and girls to meet me with several sponsors previously appointed by the pastor, in a side room and I would talk to them about their part in the series of meetings. I would encourage them to pray for the visiting minister, the pastor and the church; to help with the singing and to bring their friends and school mates to the services each night. It is surprising the enthusiasm that they would generate in the meetings.

In more recent years in my services I would use one or two choice young people to bring a testimony each night. The pastor and I would get a select group around the table and we would assign certain general topics for them to emphasize in their testimonies. This has proved to be a great blessing not only to the young people but to the community at large. Jesus' method of reaching the individual through the eye gate can be used in all revival services, in the regular worship service and by Sunday school teachers and all leaders of youth.

I have prepared this volume as a source book for those who work with young people who need suggestions for their programs and messages. It is my prayer that it will be of service to both young and old.

H. W. Connelly

Contents

1

A Dollar Bill

During the song service on the opening night of a series of meetings, usually after the boys and girls have sung a special number, the pastor will say, "Our guest minister has a special message for the boys, girls and young people. Each night in his own way he will use an object to teach them some helpful lessons. He will now bring his first lesson."

I would stand and greet cheerfully the young groups and say something like this, "When Jesus was on earth, he often used simple objects to illustrate his deep spiritual truths. They were always interesting and familiar to the people. His lessons were so simple, yet profound and practical, that every time you saw one of these objects you would think of the truth he revealed about it. I am persuaded that this is the best way to teach.

"Each night I am going to ask you to bring me something to talk about. I was not here to tell you what to bring tonight so I am going to use this object. At the close of the service I will tell you what to bring tomorrow night. What is this, boys and girls?" They always respond quickly, "A dollar bill." "Yes, that is right. This is a dollar bill. This is coined personality. There is something sacred about it. The Bible tells us that the earth is the Lord's. That the silver and the gold are his, therefore, to whom does this dollar belong? You are right, it belongs to God. It is in my possession to use for God's glory but in the last analysis it belongs to Him. It took a lot of hard work for me to get possession of this dollar."

Then I begin to crumple it up in my hand, throw it out in the aisle and say, "What do you think of a fellow who works hard to earn the dollar and then throws it away?" Pausing for a reply, I would soon hear one of them say, "I think he is crazy," or something like that.

I agree, as the congregation smiles. "Boys and girls, it is a sin to waste. Jesus said after feeding the 5,000 to gather up the fragments. Let nothing be wasted. But we Americans are said to be the greatest wasters in the world. We waste enough food to feed the rest of the hungry world. Our annual crime, drink and gambling bills would build churches, schools and hospitals all over the world to bless people. All of this is worse than wasted. Then, boys and girls, we burn up billions of dollars in cigarette smoking and now they tell us that the cigarette has a substance that will cause cancer of the lungs. I visited a man this week who had a strong vigorous body but he was an insistent cigarette smoker. Already the doctors have taken out one lung and the other is badly damaged. His years of youthfulness have been tremendously reduced.

"I want to talk to you about another way we Christians throw away God's money. I thank God for the lovely churches which we have, but how foolish it is to erect costly buildings and carry on expensive programs and then not attend the services. One of the most costly things about a church is an empty pew. If you want to know its value, add up the cost of the building, equipment and the current expenses of the church, divide by the number of pews, and you will find how much an empty pew costs. Let's fill up our cars with passengers as we come to church each night that we might have all the pews filled with worshipers. Now will you hand me that dollar bill that I threw into the aisle? I don't want to be a waster."

2

A Hammer

Our preacher for tonight is in this paper bag and I shall present him at this time. (Holding up the hammer) This is Rev. Mr. Hammer. He has a message for you boys and girls."

1. He said, " Tell the boys and girls that I am the only knocker worth anything. Leave all the knocking to me. That is what I am made for." There are some people who go through life knocking others. They will knock the officers of the land, knock the school teachers, the preachers and churches but they don't get very far in life. We are not to make our light burn brighter by dimming someone elses light." I was visiting in a nice home some time ago and the lady of the house said, "I want you to see my floor in the upstairs hallway." The house had beautiful hardwood floors and as we reached the top of the stairway there was a place about a yard square that was beaten into splinters. I said to her, "How did this happen?" She said, "You know Juanita. She got mad and sat there on the floor with a hammer and beat a hole in it." That took a lot of brains, didn't it?

2. Again Rev. Hammer says, "I am not only a knocker, I am a puller, but I cannot pull and knock at the same time. As a puller I have to stop knocking and if I knock I have to stop pulling." That is true in life. You will find the chronic knockers are not pullers and you will find that the pullers do not have time to knock. We want to join the group of pullers and pull for our church and Sunday school and for our country.

3. Mr. Hammer said, "I keep my head. I don't fly off the handle." It is a dangerous thing to fly off the handle. I went to a flourishing town some time ago to hold a series of meetings. We started on Monday night. As we walked out on the pulpit platform I noticed an old man sitting to my right with his left hand slightly elevated and his thumb was bandaged and looked as

large as my fist. Every time I turned to the right I saw that thumb. He left the building before I could speak to him and find out his trouble. The following day the pastor said, "We shall go up to Brother Blanks today." As we walked up on the porch the door opened and out walked that thumb. I said, "Brother, what happened to that thumb?" He replied, "I was nailing up my fence around the back yard and my hammer flew off the handle, struck my thumb and broke it. I have suffered terribly with it." I said, "That was a bad hammer to play a trick like that on you." Don't you know there are lots of people who fly off the handle and do lots of harm.

I go into various parts of the state in my work and find churches and Sunday schools that have grown rapidly and then occasionally find somebody flies off the handle and tears them to pieces. Boys and girls, let's learn now to keep our heads and not fly off the handle. The Bible says, "He that ruleth his own spirit is greater than he that takes a city."

4. Mr. Hammer says, "I am a builder." I said, "Well, Mr. Hammer, that is my business too." I am in the biggest building business in the world. I am building a life and that is your business too, boys and girls. You are to build a life. Thomas Jefferson was asked one time what he was going to make of himself. He said, "I am going to try to make a man and if I fail in that, I won't be anything." Do you know what is the most important thing about a building? It is the foundation. I don't care how much pains you may take erecting a building, if you don't have a good foundation it just won't stand. That same thing is true in life. We must have a good foundation. The Bible says there is just one foundation that will stand the storm. That is Jesus. He is the chief cornerstone. If you will open your hearts and receive Him as your Saviour and Lord and build upon that foundation your building will stand the storm. I hope you will receive Him tonight and build your life upon Him. Let us stand and sing "On Christ, the solid rock I stand, All other ground is sinking sand."

3

What to Take to School Each Day

I didn't ask anyone to bring me an object to talk about because I am going to talk about five things and I want you to guess what they are. (They will give me answers like books, pencils, paper, lunch.) I am thinking about something even more important.

1. Take an open mind. Trust your teacher and work with her. Remove all prejudice and learn to get the viewpoint of others. There are two sides to all questions. Train yourself to see both sides. Maybe you have been wrong in your thinking.

2. Take a desire to learn. You are now working for your future. An old man, in speaking of some people who went West in search of gold, said, "They have the desire but they are lacking in the digging principle." Don't expect the teacher to chew and digest the food for you, but learn to do that yourselves. Jesus said, "Blessed are those that hunger and thirst for they shall be filled." You are not educated by the teacher pouring knowledge into your head, but by solving your problem yourselves.

3. Take a willingness to work with others, even those you don't especially like. That is a real need today. President Johnson was asked, "What is America's greatest problem today?" He replied, "It is learning to live with others." The school is a good place to learn this lesson. I knew a very capable young man who could do most anything he wanted to do but he could not work with others and consequently he didn't advance very far.

4. Carry a smile. The wise man said, "A merry heart doeth good as medicine." It helps you and it blesses others. Greet your teachers and fellow pupils with a cheery "Good Morning." It will help to dispel the gloom of the day. A teacher, speaking of a certain student, said, "She is the most radiant Christian I have ever known. You will never know what her smile has meant to this school."

5. Carry a determination to stick to your problem until it is solved. You will meet problems all through life and school is

a good place to learn to conquer them. There was an eminent minister, P. S. Henson, who lived in Boston. He was invited to bring the commencement address at Richmond College. All were wondering about what the learned Doctor would speak. He arose and said, "My subject is 'Stick, YES, STICK.'" He drove home to the audience the importance of sticking to the task on hand until it is finished.

This is a day of "drop outs." Boys, girls and young people are dropping out of school. Our leaders are disturbed about it. There were two boys in high school who decided they would quit and go to work and make money. One was going to work in a drug store and the other was going to drive a truck. The first boy returned home and told his preacher father what he planned to do. The wise father talked with his son and explained to him how he would be crippled in life if he didn't complete his education and the boy returned to school the next day. The second boy told his father his plans. The father said, "Son, I am sending you to school for your own good. If you don't want to go but prefer to work, I will set you up in business." He wanted to drive a truck, and the father bought him a truck and a horse. In a year's time the first boy was graduating from high school. The second boy was driving his truck. In four years the first boy was graduating from college with high honors. The other boy was driving his truck. In a few years the first boy was elected President of Princeton University and his life was touching those young people who were going out to be world leaders. The other boy was driving his truck. In a few years, the first boy was elected Governor of the state of New Jersey. The second boy was driving his truck. In a few years the nation felt they needed a man of ideals to be President of this nation and the first boy was elected to the high office and filled it with a great distinction. He lead the nation through one of its greatest wars and went to the peace table with ideals and principles that were destined to influence the world. The other boy was still driving his truck. Who was this first boy? Woodrow Wilson, of course. Suppose Mr. Wilson had dropped out of school during the high school period. Look what a loss the world would have sustained.

4

The Mission of a Mirror

1. The mirror will give you back whatever you give it. You walk up before a mirror and give it a smile, it will smile back at you. If you give it a frown, it will frown back at you. Someone has said, "The man who invented the mirror made a valuable contribution to civilization." Charles Daniel from Richmond, Virginia, had the habit of walking up before a mirror each morning and saying to himself, "Old fellow, this is a new day, why not make the most of it?"

2. What is the oldest mirror? Do you know who made the first mirror? God made a lake and that is a mirror. You know if you look into a lake you can see yourself. I heard the story of a dog that started across a body of water walking on a log with a bone in his mouth. He looked into the water and saw a dog and a bone down there. He turned his bone loose and dived head foremost into the water after the bone. Do you know what happened? He lost his bone. That frequently happens with greedy people who go after what belongs to others.

3. The earth is like a mirror. The Bible says, "Whatsoever a man soweth, that shall he reap." You give the earth a watermelon seed and it will give you back a melon. You give it a grain of corn and you don't get back a grain of wheat, but corn. The Bible says, "The seed brings forth after its kind." The earth returns to you what it gets from you.

4. A life is like a mirror. It gives you what you give it. A little boy was out on a hill playing and when he yelled, he heard a boy on the other hill yell back. He said, "I hate you" and the other little boy said, "I hate you." He said, "I'll get you" and the other little boy said "I'll get you." So the little boy ran and told his mother about the little boy on the other hill saying "I hate you" so the mother said "Now, you go back to the same spot and say to that little boy, 'I love you' and see if he doesn't

say, 'I love you'." That is true of life. We get what we give.

5. You give life your best and it will give the best back to you. You give it a smile and it will smile back. It was said of Philips Brooks, the great Boston preacher, that he could not walk down the street and not bring a blessing to everybody he passed. His personality inspired them and he was blessed by their response.

5

A Small and a Large Potato

In this brown bag we have two preachers for tonight. Let me present them to you now. These are the Reverends "Tater." The interesting thing about them is that they are brothers. They lived in the same house, slept in the same bed, ate from the same table but just look how much bigger and finer this one is than that one. I asked this little runt why he was not a big fine preacher like his brother. He said, "I didn't start soon enough." That is the way with lots of people. They don't get started soon enough. It is better to start the Christian life late than not to start at all, but it is so much better to begin in the morning of life while you are boys and girls. I came to Christ as a boy and gave my life to him as well as my soul.

2. Then this little fellow said, "I didn't have room over on my side of the house to grow. There were rocks, weeds and grass that crowded me out." The same is true today with many people. They let other things crowd them out. Let's empty our lives of all bad habits and make room in our hearts for Jesus.

3. This little fellow said, "You know, I didn't have the right sort of food to make me like my big brother," and again that is often true of many people today. They don't feed on the wholesome food to nourish their bodies.

Walking down the street one day, I saw a little girl approaching. She was weak and pale and her little eyes were set back in her head. Her teeth were decayed and she was the picture of under-nourishment. I asked her name and where she lived and she told me. Then I asked where she went to Sunday school and she replied, "I don't go anywhere." I asked if she drank much milk and she replied, "I don't drink milk at all." I asked what they drank and she replied, "We drink beer." I was not surprised at her weak emaciated body when I learned on what she fed. Some boys and girls are starving their bodies by feeding on that which is harmful rather than taking good nourishing food. The same is true of our spiritual lives. They don't take nourishing spiritual vitamins. Which would you rather be—a fine preacher like this one or a little runt like that? (All replied "I would rather be like the big fine one.") I know you would so let's make up our minds today and start by accepting Jesus, and putting out of our lives all that would injure us and feed our souls on the spiritual vitamins of God's word.

6

A Pile of Potatoes

Thank you boys and girls for this nice pile of potatoes. You have all sorts and sizes here, and my friend John brought along a sweet potato as I suggested for him to do. I am going to pick out five of these to be our preachers for tonight.

1. You will notice this one has a lot of specks on it. I call him a speck "tater." You know what a speck "tater" is. He represents a group that sits on the side lines and doesn't play nor root for the team. The church has too many members like that today. They don't do anything and they usually criticize those that are trying. This type never gets anywhere in life. When Jesus came to the fig tree expecting to find fruit but found only leaves, he killed the tree and it was uprooted and thrown out of the garden. Let's not disappoint Jesus with a fruitless life.

2. These two are almost exactly alike. I call them imi"taters." An "imitater" is one that just follows the crowd—when in Rome, do as the Romans do—no convictions, no standard. We don't want to be different, just to be different and peculiar, but we need to exercise the power of choice and have a standard. I heard of a lovely girl who entered the University and, being a pretty girl, all the boys wanted to date her. They asked to take her to the dance, the cocktail party, or some such place and she would reply politely and say "I don't go to such places." One of her suitors said to her, "You are going to ruin your college life. You will be considered a stick in the mud and you will have no friends if you don't go along with us to these places." But at the end of the session, her picture was hung on the wall and underneath was written, "The most popular girl in school." You don't have to lower your standard to be popular, but like this girl let's try to lift our associates up to our standard.

3. This little "tater" I call the comment"tater." He has the

happy faculty of talking all the time and always saying the wrong thing. He just doesn't count.

4. This big one, I call a dic"tater." He has to be always in the lead or he won't play. He is like the fellow the Apostle John tells about in his third epistle. He always has to have the pre-eminence. He sits on the platform and tries to look wise but is not called on to participate.

5. This is one that everybody loves. This is the sweet "tater." Listen, boys and girls, you can always catch more flies with molasses than you can with vinegar. The world needs happy and helpful people. Let's develop a sweet spirit and a radiant personality so we may help others along the way of life.

Don't you think it would be nice to give all these "taters" to our pastor's wife and ask her to make him some "tater" soup? All in favor say "I."

7

Four Ears of Corn

You will notice each of these ears of corn are different in color. This is white, this very dark, this is red and this one is yellow. They all grew in the same field and they are all of the same substance and are of equal value but they are different in appearance.

We find here a timely lesson. God is the maker of all four of these ears of corn and they are, I am sure, all precious to him regardless of their color.

The human family its made up of four colors of people. We have the white, black, red and yellow. All are made by the same God and are, I am sure, of equal value to him.

Let's turn in our Bible to Acts 17:26 and read what it says, "God hath made of one blood all nations of men for to dwell on all the face of the earth."

The scientists tell us they can take blood from different animals of the earth and put it through tests and tell it is different. But they cannot detect any difference between blood of the different colors of the races. All are human beings. All are made by God, have the same desires and similar needs. They are all lost without Christ. All can be saved by trusting in him. All will be judged. All will have to give an account of their stewardship of all phases of life. Then all should have equal opportunities of life. In thinking of this question, I try to put myself in their shoes. I was born white, but suppose I had been born a yellow or black boy. How would I feel today about this question. It is no fault or credit to me to be white. I did not choose my color. Neither did those of a different color choose their color. Therefore, it is wrong for us because we are in the majority in our community to take advantage of those in minority.

When you take the whole human race the white people are very much in the minority. If we, through superior advantages, have gone further than the others, it is our responsibility to try to provide equal advantage to them and lift them to the highest level possible.

There is a little chorus that we often sing, "Jesus loves the little children, all the children of the world. Red and yellow, black and white, they are precious in his sight; Jesus loves the little children of the world."

8

The Stamp

Boys and girls, I am not a stamp collector but I asked all of you to bring me a stamp tonight and I promised to tell you something about them. When I finish with them I am going to lay them on the table and each of you come and get your stamp at the close of the service. So now each of you come forward and lay your stamp in my hand. Thank you, thank you very much. You can always count on the boys and girls. Now, raising my hands before the congregation I said, "Look at the stamps. Notice the different kinds and colors. I am going to lay them on the table and take just one for my subject tonight. The first thing I notice, boys and girls is that Mr. Stamp carries his value on his face. That is true of each of you. You can look at a boy or girl and pretty well tell their value. Truth will out. Whatever is within you is revealed in your face.

I was in a strange city one time and saw an article in a store window that I wanted but I did not have the cash to buy it. I stepped inside and said to the clerk, "I would like to purchase that article there, but I do not have the cash with me to pay for it. If you will accept my check, I'll take it." "I think we can handle that," he replied, and walked back into the office. Out walked a stern, handsome man whom, I am sure, was the store manager. He merely glanced out of the corner of his eye at me and turned to the clerk and said, "Go ahead and accept his check." Experience had taught him to read character by looking at you.

2. The stamp's business is to carry a message. They carry messages all over the world. There are homesick boys across the sea in the service of Uncle Sam who are longing for Mr. Stamp to bring them a message from home. Now you and I are here to carry a message. That is our main business. We work in the store, on the farm, in the factory to pay expenses but our main

job is to witness for Christ. He wants you boys and girls to tell others about him.

Sitting on my porch one day in Newport News, Virginia, I saw a lovely little girl, about ten years of age, walking by my home. I spoke to her and asked her name and where she lived. Then I asked where she attended Sunday school. She said she didn't go anywhere because her mother was dead and she had to keep house for her father and in order to get to school she had to work lots on Sunday. I asked her if she would like to come to Sunday school and her face lightened up and she said, "I surely would." The following Sunday she was in Sunday school and in a few Sundays she came forward accepting Christ as her Saviour. A few Sundays after that I noticed a strange lady sitting by her in church and when the invitation was given the lady came forward making a profession of faith in Christ. When the service was over, little Lois ran up to me and said, "I told her about Jesus and brought her to church today." The lady reached down and put her arms around the little ten year old girl and said, "Yes, Lois lives next door to me and she has been telling me about her church and Saviour and it is through her that I am here today." You can tell your neighbors about Jesus and let them know him too.

3. Mr. Stamp is no good as a messenger until he is cancelled out. You have to give him a licking and a sticking. He must be attached to be used. If God is to use you as his messengers you have to cancel out self and become attached to Jesus and enlist in your church as a representative. Why don't you take this step tonight?

9

A Rose

As you approach the end of this message, pull the petals off the rose as you talk, showing how quickly the rose can be destroyed.

Boys and girls, this is the best looking preacher we have had in the pulpit this week. Who made this rose? Certainly, God made it. And he had a purpose in making it. He wanted this world, which is our temporary home, to be a beautiful place to live. He planted the roses, made the birds, the mountains and lakes to make the world more attractive. Who made you, boys and girls? Yes, God. He had a purpose in making you. He wants you to contribute your part to make this world beautiful. He loves the good and beautiful. What is more beautiful than bright, happy groups of boys and girls. It hurts our Heavenly Father for us to be ugly and do wrong, but he is pleased when we are good and happy.

It took God a long time to make this rose. Last winter this was an ugly root and he gradually unfolded its beauty and scattered its fragrance all around. God takes time and does well what he wants to do. I remember one day, during my first pastorate, of sitting on the front porch talking with one of the deacons of the church. We were discussing the huge oak tree standing in the corner of the yard. It was round and tall. Its limbs reached some twenty feet in all directions. He said, "That tree is over one hundred years old. It was a good sized tree when I moved here as a little boy." As we were talking we heard the rumble of thunder as a big cloud was gathering in the West. It came closer and closer as the wind was pushing hard against it. In a little while, the rain began and we had to move inside the house. In a few moments there was a keen streak of lightning that hit the top of that tree and knocked it into a thousand splinters in a split second. I remember there was an old rooster that had sought shelter under the tree during the storm and he was lying cold in death with both eyes open after the storm had passed. He didn't have time to close his eyes. It took God a century to make that tree but it was destroyed in the batting of an eye. It takes a long time to build a life but you can destroy it through dissipation, in a very short time. You can wreck your life, as I have wrecked this flower, as I was talking to you. Let us always remember that our lives are given us by God, pure and precious to Him, and us, therefore, let us not carelessly wreck it along the journey.

I heard of a young man who was reared in a good home but he got with the wrong crowd and decided one night that he would take a fling. He went out with the crowd and in one night of revelry he caught a disease that quickly sapped his life and sent him into a premature grave. Your life is sacred, therefore, link it to God and live for him.

10

Weeds and Bad Habits

Weeds are like bad habits.

1. Both start from small beginnings. A tiny little seed so small you can scarcely see it will start a weed. Bad habits, likewise, have small beginnings but they grow.

2. Neither have to be cultivated. To grow pretty flowers, you have to prepare and fertilize the soil and work and water the plants but the weeds will flourish anywhere in most any kind of soil. Good habits have to be cultivated to grow. They require self-discipline and patient repetition.

3. Weeds and bad habits will multiply. Drop a seed this year and you will get a bunch of weeds and next year they will produce a field of weeds. Often one bad habit leads to another, and if you take something that doesn't belong to you, you will soon have to be telling a lie to cover it up.

4. They are both hardy and strong. The weeds are the first plants that come up in the spring and the last to die in the fall. They stand the drought and heat.

5. Lastly the longer you let them go the harder they are to get rid of. You had better nip them in the bud or you will have a hard time getting rid of them. Jesus gave us strength to overcome our weakness and bad habits. Let him enter your heart while you are young and give up those things that would injure your character.

11

Some Lessons from a Honey Bee

I asked, privately, a boy to draw me a picture of the Honey Bee which I used as my Object Lesson. The Honey Bee is one of the most helpful, interesting and suggestive creatures that we have. His worthy traits, if emulated will make us better Christians. The first lesson I draw from him is that he is an industrious creature. You hear the expression, "busy as a bee." The bee is busy. He works from light to dark during his busy season. You will recall it was said of Jesus, "He was always going about doing good." He said, "My Father works hitherto and I work." Our Heavenly Father wants us to be busy in his vineyard.

2. The Honey Bee goes straight. You hear the expression, "straight as a bee line." The little busy fellow flies away to the flower gardens or to the blooming trees and loads up with honey and rises up to the level of his home. Then goes like a bullet straight to his home. Speaking geometrically we would say, "A straight line is the shortest distance between two points." He loses no time just floundering around.

3. The Honey Bee knows how to divide responsibilities among themselves. They have their separate duties to perform. Some are watchmen. You disturb them and the same ones will come out and investigate the disturbance. If you are meddling around his home you had better watch for soon he will have all the guards on your neck, if you don't get out of their way. Others have the responsibility of chiseling out the honey and sticking it to their legs and bringing it home. When he arrives all out of breath, he falls on the floor of the bee gum and another helper collects it and packs it away in the top, so each one has his respective task to fulfill.

4. They are loyal to their leaders. They will follow the queen and they dare not practice insubordination. Woe unto the soldier

who strays away from the army. They don't tolerate drones. If one gets lazy and refuses to work he is taken to the door and kicked out.

5. The Honey Bee spends his time making life sweet. If all Christians were as concerned, about making life sweet and attractive, as is the Honey Bee, we would have a different world. The bee is wise. He prepares for the future. He lays up in the summer for the cold winter months. If this creature can look ahead and get ready for tomorrow, shouldn't we see the importance of the future? The Bible says, "Prepare to meet thy God." We get ready by receiving Christ as our Saviour and Lord and enlisting our lives in his church for worship, service and growth.

12

The Ants

In Proverbs 6:6-8 the wise man said "Go to the ant, thou sluggard; consider her ways, and be wise, which have no ruler, overseer or guide, provides her meat in summer." Solomon is here speaking to the sluggards who love ease and idleness and have no business about them. He sends the sluggard to school. The sluggard will not voluntarily go to the wise teacher of vision so he sends him to the humbles insects. Go to the ants, bees, spiders and learn their ways. Man who is made a little lower than the angels but with his superior faculties can degenerate beneath the lowest insects and beasts of the forest.

The ants do not make war on each other and exterminate their race but as we will learn they will provide for themselves and help their neighbors.

It says to consider their ways. The sluggards do not consider. They only think of today. They make no plans for the rainy day and for old age. Consider and be wise. Wisdom is higher than knowledge. If they drop out from school and those who never look ahead would stop and think where they will land if they continue in their loose, careless way of living, they would change their course. The Psalmist said, "I thought on my way turned my feet unto thy testimonies."

The ant will build him a house and then go out in the heat of summer, gather in the harvest and store it away for the winter. If he finds his neighbor trying to drag a big bug to his home, he will lend a helping hand. They have no guides, overseers to tell but instinct teaches them how to act.

As thinking creatures we should go a step further and consider. There is an eternity before us and there is but one of two places to spend it. Then if we have learned anything from the ants we would prepare for it by accepting Christ and serving him.

13

A Lump of Salt

This evening we have one of the most common things in life that has a message for all of us. The lump of salt. While it is very common and cheap it is essential to life. Man nor beast can live without it. Let us examine some of its leading qualities. In the first place, it is a preserver of life. In preparing meat for food, we put salt on it to preserve it. Jesus said, "Ye are the salt of the earth," therefore, we are to preserve life in the community where we live. To do this we must contact the people around us. You may have your cellar full of salt and your smokehouse full of meat but unless the salt contacts the meat it will not help preserve it. I have helped to start a number of churches. One of the most interesting parts of the work to me is to make contact with people in the community. In preparing the meat for future use, the farmer takes the hog and cuts it into pieces and pours on the salt and rubs it in. The salt must penetrate the bone to save the meat. If we are to save society we must penetrate to the depths, those around us, and instill in them the message of life. Salt not only preserves food but seasons it. Did you ever try to eat an egg without any salt? Pretty flat, isn't it? You and I are to season life wherever we go. To live in a pagan land where there is no spiritual salt to add flavor to life, must be a dry and monotonous experience. But do you know there are communities right in the good old U.S.A. like that? It is our task to evangelize them. Just fail to evangelize one generation and you have a pagan community. When Jesus said, "Ye are the salt of the earth," he also went on to say that when salt has lost its savor, it is good for nothing but to be cast out and be trodden under the foot of man. It is only good to stop up gulleys and to walk on. When the seasoning and purifying effect of the salt is gone it has no value. How true is that of you and me. There are thousands of people whose names are on the church roll who have lost their savor. They have no purifying, preserving and seasoning effect. Paul warned against this sort of life when he said, "I beat my body blue to keep it in subjection, lest when I preach to others, I, myself shall be a castaway." There is before me an old fountain pen that has lost its usefulness. It is just a castaway. Let us watch and pray and be alert and not become a castaway.

14

Three Pencils

I hold in my hand, three pencils. These look alike but they are different. They are all the same size, same length and color but one of these pencils is more valuable than the other two. What do you think makes them different? That's right. It is the quality of the lead. The lead in this pencil is too hard. It doesn't make the right impression on the paper. I don't enjoy writing with it. There are people like that. Their hearts are too hard to be used in Christ's service. They have not received Jesus as their Saviour, therefore, their hearts are hard. Did you ever think about it? The same sun that melts snow will harden mortar and the same gospel that will save if accepted will harden if rejected. The Bible says, "Today if you will hear my voice, harden not your heart." I believe God uses the best prepared person who is close to him.

This pencil is no good because it is too soft. When you try to write it makes a broad smutty line that messes up the paper. It will not penetrate into the paper and last. Many people are too soft for service. They need to be purified and tempered to have the enduring quality.

Now, this pencil is just right and I love to use it. All I have to do is to keep it sharp and guide it as it should go. Trimming a pencil is like pruning a tree. It is more valuable after you prepare it for service. There is another lesson that we should learn from the pencil. We can change the mark of the pencil by using a rubber that will erase the message, but when you do that you have marred the paper. It just doesn't look quite as neat. It is so much better to write it down correctly and not have to erase. We are told that our lives are like a book. That is, we write a page each day and we should seek to make the message clear and plain. In his infinite love for us, God has made it possible for us to be forgiven of our blunders and sins. There is a little chorus which says, "God has blotted them out, I am happy and glad and free. God has blotted them out, I will turn to Isaiah and see, Chapter 44:22 and 23. He blotted them out and now I can shout for that means me."

We do thank God for his forgiving grace but we should strive to live purer each day so that we will not be scarred by sin. Yes, we want to be good, but we want to be good for something. By trusting and following Jesus and by improving ourselves in every way possible, we can be of service to him and to mankind.

15

A Pin

What is this in my hand, boys and girls? Yes, this is a pin. He is the smallest preacher who has been in the pulpit this week, but you cannot tell the worth of a preacher by his physical size.

I want you to notice that this pin is perfectly straight. Have you ever tried to use a crooked pin? It just won't hold. You cannot depend on it. The same is true of a crooked boy or girl. You can't trust them. I like to see boys and girls that are straight in body. Sit up straight. Now you look better. You want also to think straight. The Bible says, "As as man thinks on in his heart so is he." The deeds pass through the mind before they are performed. If we will learn to think straight we will also act straight.

It never pays to do wrong. When our boy was about ten years old we took him to Washington and through the big government buildings. When the guide was taking us through the building showing us how we catch criminals he kept saying to the group, "Crime doesn't pay. Go out and tell the public that crime doesn't pay." When we finished the tour and came back to the entrance of the building, our son dashed out of the door and ran over to where his mother was sitting under a tree. He said, "Mother, I learned one thing, crime doesn't pay." We felt well repaid for the expense of the trip.

You will notice this pin has a point. Did you ever try to use a pin with a broken point? There is a point to a successful life. There is one essential. It is to be a Christian. Take Christ into your life. He will help you to think straight and to act straight because you will be straight if he is in your life.

In the last place you will observe that the pin has a head. This is always an important part of the body. Tell me what is the difference between this head and your head. Yes, it's smaller.

No, it has no eyes nor mouth. What other difference? No brains. That is what I wanted you to say. The pin has no mind and it cannot choose. God has given you a brain so you can think and make choices in life. And it is so important, boys and girls to make wise choices. We choose the places we go, the things we do, the people with whom we associate. Now the most important of all of life's choices is to choose a Saviour. We are going to need him. We need him now. So why not open your heart tonight and say, "Lord Jesus, I need you and I love you. Come into my heart and make me what you want me to be."

16

A Knife and a Razor

Both of these instruments are used for cutting purposes but there is a vast difference between the two. This knife is strong and sharp but it is used for rough material. While this razor is used only for cutting hair. The difference is in the quality of material out of which it is made. This razor has high class steel and it is highly tempered. You and I are made of the same kind of material. We have capacities for high development. The important thing is to develop. If you will grind the axe you will chop more wood. If you will sharpen the razor you will find it will cut, but you just try to shave with a dull razor. It will test your religion.

We are tempered and sharpened by our contacts with people. That is why you go to school, to Sunday school and church. It is to prepare you for service. You are tempered by your enduring hardships and trials. Job said, "I am being tried and I will come forth as gold."

There has doubtless never been a time when education was so important as now. Everything is specialized. One has to be a specialist in something to get employment today. And it is going to be more evident tomorrow. John A. Broadus, a noted educator of the last generation used to say to his pupils, "Young gentlemen, know something about everything but be sure to know everything about something." Abraham Lincoln said, "I am going to get ready and maybe my time will come." Your time will come if you prepare for it. Let's discipline our lives and sharpen the blade for tomorrow's task.

17

A River

In describing any country one will tell you about the rivers. In his writings about our Heavenly home, the inspired Apostle John said, in the Revelation, "He showed me a river." I want you to think about the value of a river, tonight, as we draw some lessons from it.

1. Rivers enrich and purify the country through which they pass. Farm lands on the river are far more valuable than those in the hills. They have a way of overflowing the banks occasionally and depositing debris over the soil that enriches the land and takes away impurities. You and I should seek to enrich the lives of those with whom we daily come in contact. Someone has said, "The part of our religion that overflows is what blesses others." Tennyson said, "I am part of all I have met." It is an inspiring thought that we can contribute something to everyone with whom we come in contact.

2. Rivers carry burdens on their bosoms. My old teacher used to tell us that one is valuable in proportion to his ability to carry burdens. Paul said, "Bear ye one another's burdens." A good motto for life is to pull your own weight and try to carry someone else's load who is unable to bear it.

3. Rivers furnish power for running machinery. The higher and narrower the banks, the more power the river has. Jesus commended to us the straight and narrow way. He doesn't mean by that, that we are to live small lives cutting ourselves off from others, but it is really the reverse. The high, deep life of power is the happy and useful life. The Christian is the one who lives the abundant life.

4. Rivers have periods of prosperity and depression. We also find that is common with us. We cannot stay on the mountain top all the time. Some days we have to spend in the valley. I

heard a wise teacher say, "Never make an important decision when you are in the dumps."

5. Rivers feed from above. If they did not they would soon dry up and that is the way we are. We need new strength for each day and I am thankful to tell you that God's reservoir is full and inexhaustible. There is no danger that his blessing will give out. He says, "My grace is sufficient for thee." In speaking of God's abundance, Mr. Spurgeon said, "Some people remind me of a mouse on a mountain top that is afraid to draw a long breath for fear there would not be any air left for tomorrow."

6. Rivers always reach their destination. You can dam them up and delay their progress but you cannot defeat them. Ultimately they will reach the sea. Man can delay the progress of the Kingdom but man cannot defeat God. "The Kingdoms of this world shall become the Kingdom of our Lord."

18

Beans Will Come Up

A little boy ran in and asked his father if he could go fishing. His father replied, "Not today son, we must plant our beans." "But" replied the little boy, "all the boys from school are going and I want to go too." "Yes" replied the father, "but we must plant our beans." "Well," persisted the boy, "may I go fishing after we plant the beans?" "Yes," replied the father. So the boy picked up the bucket of beans and off to the farm he went and began dropping the beans, two to a hill. After several rows he looked into the bucket and he could scarcely miss the beans, so he began to drop three to a hill and finally four then he began to drill them. Getting down near the bottom he raised the bucket and throwing it he scattered the beans as far as he could and he dropped the bucket and joined the boys over on the creek bank.

In about three weeks the father said, "Son, let's go down to the farm and see if the beans have come up." It was the first time the boy had thought about the beans coming up. He followed after his father down the path, wondering what the field would look like. Arriving at the bean patch, the father said, "Yes, son, they are coming up all right. Two in a hill just as I told you." Going further on the father said, "Well, here is three in the hill and there is four." Coming to where the boy drilled them and where he threw the bucket out, it looked as if the whole surface of the earth was lifted with beans. The father stood in silence looking at the beans while the little fellow stood trembling behind him. Then the father turned around, caught the little fellow by the hand and dropped on his knees praying this prayer, "Oh, Lord, I don't mind wasting the beans if you will teach my boy that beans will come up." The boy learned a valuable lesson that day. That is "Whatsoever you sow, you reap."

19

A Ball

The first lesson I get from the ball is that it has no end. You will notice it is round. If an ant starts to crawl to the end and jump off he would keep crawling. Life is like that. It has no end. It is true that we come to an end of this earthly life but we enter eternity. This life is important as it prepares us for the longer and richer life with Jesus.

This ball tells me it is hard to go up but easy to come down. It takes the force of my arm to throw it up but it drops back of its own weight. Again that is a lesson of life. Anybody can drift down stream but it requires effort to go up stream. One of life's great temptations is just to drift along with the tide. Take the course of least resistance, but we cannot build character like that or get very far in life. You cannot drift up stream. Progress requires a struggle.

Mr. Ball says, "I am always on the winning side." Did you ever think about it? You cannot win in any game without the ball. If the opposing team manages to keep the ball, regardless of what game you are playing, they will win. Now we want our boys and girls to win in the great game of life so we must all know and obey the rules of the game and play to the best of our ability.

The last thing Mr. Ball told me is that the unmpire always keeps his eyes on him. Regardless of the game, whether baseball, football, tennis, volley ball or whatever, you want to remember the umpire.

There was a young athlete in college whose father was blind. The father had never seen his son, who was a star player, play. The father died and was buried. The next game the son played, he outdid himself. They never saw him play so good. At the close of the game his team mates were slapping him on the back, and praising him for his superior playing and asked him why was it that he did so well. He replied, "You know, my father never saw me play because he was blind. I felt that now, he had a new pair of eyes and was watching this game and saw me play."

The Bible says, "The eyes of the Lord are in every place, keeping watch over the evil and the good." It should inspire all of us to do our best since we realize that we have a loving Father who knows us individually, watching over us and providing for our every need.

20

The Onion

1. This is not a very popular preacher. Many people do not like him. However, he has his place among the preachers for our purpose and we shall take a look at him today. The first virtue that I mention regarding him, is that he is a hardy preacher. He has qualities of endurance. You know he thrives best when you plant him in the fall and give him a chance to battle against the snow and Jack Frost. Creatures of less courage would droop and die at the first nip of cold, but not so my onion. In writing to young Timothy the veteran Paul said, "Endure hardness as good soldiers of Jesus Christ." Handicaps and hardships have their place in the molding of character. In your training for service in Uncle Sam's army they first try to toughen you to face hardships. They endeavor to get you to dedicate yourself for life to live and die for the flag of the nation. Is'nt that what Jesus was seeking to do with his army when he said that "He that taketh not his cross and followeth after me cannot be my disciple"? We are to deny self and put his cause first.

2. The Rev. Mr. Onion doesn't try to be popular by appealing to you with sweet fragrance like a rose, but often has his audience in tears as they contact each other. We should be kind to people but at the same time we will get further in life by being natural. Fill the place for which you are made, rather than try to be somebody else. I would say that the chief service the onion can render is to season other things. It improves the taste of its neighbor vegetables. He is also valuable for medicinal purposes. Our fathers used to make poultices of him and put on the chest of the children when they had colds. There are properties in him that helps to keep the body healthy and strong.

Rev. Mr. Onion is satisfied to be himself. He does not try to win friends by spreading fragrance like a rose. You don't see the suitor going about with a bouquet of onions on the lapel of his coat. It pays to be natural. Act yourself and do not try to imitate others.

21

A Rubber Band

1. There are two kinds of people in the world. Those who push you out and those who draw you in. Some are repulsive and some attract you. You see the first kind coming and you will walk across the street to keep from meeting them. But you will walk across the street in order to meet the second kind. Jesus said, "If I be lifted up, I will draw all kinds of people unto me." We should strive to be attractive to people. A girl in the training school in Louisville prayed, "Lord, make me winsome for your sake."

2. The band only serves when it is stretched. We are told to strive to enter into the Kingdom. Jesus says, "I came not to be ministered unto but to minister." You put this band on your finger and dangle it around and it is no good. M. T. Rankin, secretary of the Baptist Foreign Mission Board, used to take a globe of the world and a rubber band on his speaking tours. He would hold up the band and say, "See how small this is? But let's put it around the world and you will see how it grows."

3. The band can hold down a big job as well as a little one. Some people are not willing to do the little things in life. If you will stop to think about it, we are not worthy of the smallest task in the Kingdom of God. We should gladly accept any position that is offered. The Bible says, "He that is faithful in the few things, I will make him ruler over the many."

A Newspaper

There are always six sections to a newspaper.

1. The front page. This is where the printer puts the most exciting news. He expects to sell his paper with what is on the front page. What do you usually find there? If there is a crime of any sort, you will find it on the front page. It seems the masses are attracted to this sort of news. Let us strive to have something good in our community each day that will be fresh, attractive and inspiring news.

2. Each paper carries a society page. It is filled with news of people. We are all interested in people. Contact with others is one way of growing. Life is enriched by our association with good people. You take ten acres of land in the heart of Roanoke and it is worth millions of dollars. If there was no one living in ten miles of it, what would be its value? Our relation with others determines values.

3. Then we have the comic page. It makes us laugh and Solomon said, "A merry heart doeth good as medicine." We need to laugh. It breaks the tension and helps the circulation of blood and the digestion of our food. "All work and no play makes Jack a dull boy."

4. We also have the sports page. Clean sports helps us to break the grind of hard work. We develop our bodies through exercise. "Jesus increased in wisdom, in stature and in favor of God and man." In other words he developed the foursquare man.

5. There is the editorial page. That page makes us think. It should make you increase in wisdom. The Bible says, "as a man thinketh in his heart so is he." The deed passes through the mind before it is performed by other parts of the body. If we

can train ourselves to think straight it will help us to live straight.

6. Lastly, there are the want ads. The Psalmist said, "One thing have I desired of the Lord, that will I seek after." What are some of your upper-desires? Is it money, popularity, position? Or is it to serve mankind and to glorify God? I heard an eleven year old girl, at a prayer meeting, say, "This year I am going to try above all else to please God." Should not that be at the top of our want list?

23

A Biscuit

I said to the boys and girls, "I am hungry. Who will bring me a biscuit tomorrow night?"

Who has the preacher for tonight? Thank you Susie. Bring him forward and let me introduce him to the audience. You have him dressed in a lovely suit. Here is the Rev. Mr. Biscuit. Now, I want you boys and girls to tell me of what this biscuit is made. They will give you some information you have never heard of before, more than likely. Now, I want to know from where these different things came. Take the flour, for instance. From where did it come? You said "the wheat." Well, from where did the wheat come? You said, "the ground." Who made the ground? God. What else did God do to produce the flour that went into the biscuit. Yes, he sent the rain and sunshine and gave you strength to cultivate the soil. If you trace the other ingredients they all go back to God. We all depend upon him. He put the elements in the soil and furnishes the climate and all the essentials for producing the bread. It all comes from God. We cannot get along without him. Jesus said, "Apart from me, you can do nothing."

Our bodies cannot live without food. Now, just as our bodies demand physical food, so our souls demand spiritual food. Jesus said, one day, "I am the bread of life." The source of spiritual life is in him. God hath given to us eternal life. This life is in the Son. He that hath the Son hath life and he that hath not the Son hath not life." We accept this life through faith in Jesus. We believe that he will save us and when we trust him, he does save us. I hope you will remember that he is the source of our eternal life.

Now, when does our body need food? Surely, it is daily. The Bible says, "Give us this day our daily bread." Your soul needs daily bread as much as your body needs it, therefore, we need him now. The Bible says, "Today is the accepted time." It is unwise to put off a step that is so vital. Won't you accept him tonight?

24

A Flashlight

The purpose of the flashlight is to light your path along life's way. It is to show us how to go. That suggests your mission and mine in life. You recall that Jesus said, "I am the light of the world." In another place he says, "As long as I am in the world, I am the light of the world but now ye are the light of the world." Jesus is still the light of the world but he is no longer in the physical body with us but he is living in his believers and therefore he is to live in us and shine through us. There is a familiar song which says, "He lives, you ask me how I know he lives, He lives within my heart."

2. For the flashlight to function it must be connected with the battery. If there is no battery there is no light. That battery to the flashlight is what Jesus is to you and me. If there is no battery there is no light in the bulb. If there is no Christ in you there is no light for the dark world.

3. That bulb is to hold and reflect the light so it must be clean. A black dirty bulb cannot function. Neither can your life or mine, unless we are clean. We can, through disobedience, quench and grieve the Spirit and we can be a hindrance. The Bible says, "If the light that is in thee be darkness how great is that darkness?"

4. The flashlight supplies light for the next step. It doesn't throw the light all the way to the end of the journey. We need God daily so God often gives us a day's supply at a time. "We are to walk by faith and not by sight." That is a way that we are to grow a stronger faith by exercising it daily.

_____ ⌐ _____ ⌐ automobile, I say, "Boys and girls, let's take
a ride. We want to have a safe trip so let's talk about the essentials of our vehicle."

1. The auto has to have power to climb hills and carry its load. It draws it from another source. We need power and the Bible says, "Power belongeth unto God." Jesus said, "Tarry in Jerusalem until ye be endued with power." Ye shall receive power after the Holy Spirit comes upon you." We need power to overcome temptation and power for service. This power is from the Holy Spirit. He is to live within us. Paul says, "Know ye not that your body is the temple of the Holy Spirit." If he is to live in us our bodies must be kept fit for him.

2. The auto needs guidance. It cannot choose its course. We likewise need guidance through life and God has provided the road map for us and the Holy Spirit is here as our interpreter. Jesus said, "When the comforter comes he will guide you into all truth."

3. The car needs oil. The machinery will soon wear out without it. It prevents friction. The machinery of the church needs oil to keep down friction. Prayer under the guidance of the Spirit supplies it. We cannot make progress unless we take the time to pray. Here is the weakness of the modern church. "Ye receive not because ye ask not."

4. It must have brakes. I would not ride in a car without brakes. There are dangerous curves, steep hills to climb and descend and rough places to go over. It is unsafe without brakes. The brakes are to the car what the Christian religion is to life. It is essential to safety. To see what a nation becomes without religion, look at Russia. There are still many religious people in Russia and they are a blessing to the nation. If the Kremlin

succeeds in stamping out religion altogether that nation will be a real menace to the safety of the world.

5. The business of the automobile is to carry loads. It transports people and things from place to place. Our business is also to carry loads. Paul said, "Bear ye one another's burdens and fulfill the law of Christ." We are not here just to have a good time and follow the road of least resistance. We, as Christians, are to take the offensive against all evil and make our contribution to our day and generation.

A Spark Plug

There are similarities between the spark plug and a Christian. Let's see what the spark plug can teach us.

1. The plug must be in place. In my garage there are a half-dozen spark plugs lying up on a shelf. They are not serving and in our churches there are hundreds of members lying up on the shelf listening to the T.V. and reading the papers while the world burns up. I heard of a returned missionary who said, "The world is looking at America and America is looking at the Television. We must arouse our churches."

2. The plug must be in contact with the battery and with the engine. We have to be in constant contact with God and with the people. The lost are all around us and we can get hardened to the fact of their lost condition. Half the people of your city will not be in church next Sunday. If they get the message somebody will have to contact them. Let those who go to them be sure they are in contact with God and have his message.

3. All the plugs must cooperate if the engine has power and runs smoothly. Did you ever drive a car when one plug is dead and feel it hesitate, jump and jerk. That reminds me of many of our members who are silent and thereby robbing the church of power and smooth running. When Pentecost came "They were all of one accord in one place."

Some of our churches need to take a group of members off the shelf, clean up and adjust them and put them in contact with God and the needy people in a growing area. It will surprise you what those on the shelf will do if you adjust them to the task.

4. Of course, the plug must be clean and adjusted or it will not fire. But let them repent and see the need and they will fire and pull and furnish power.

27

A Bunch of Keys

Here is a bunch of keys. Big keys, little keys, long keys. Each fits a certain lock. You have to have the key to fit the certain lock. Jesus said something about giving us the keys of the kingdom. Giving knowledge of his will, of his plan of salvation so we must use these keys to unlock the hearts of people to get in the message of Christ. How can we reach the hearts of the people with Christ's message?

1. Use the key of kindness. Paul said "Be kind one to another." Sitting on my porch one day I was watching the approaching storm from the West. The wind was blowing. The heavens were flashing with lightning and loud with thunder. I saw a young mother pushing a baby carriage with her baby and several bundles in it. As she hastened past my door one of the front wheels came off and ran several yards down the street. The carriage came near turning over. I rushed and grabbed the wheel and stuck it back on and slipped a nail in it where the cotter pin had come out and I said to the lady, "Won't you come in and wait until the storm is over?" She said, "Thank you, but I think I can make it to the bus before it begins to rain." About three weeks after that my phone rang and a strange lady's voice said, "My mother died last night and I would like for you to conduct her funeral tomorrow." I told her I would and that I would be over in a short time to arrange for it. As I entered the home she gave me a cordial welcome and said, "I suppose you are wondering why I, a stranger, am asking you to bury my mother. But do you remember nearly a month ago a lady with a baby carriage was rushing by your home trying to catch the bus before the storm, and a wheel came off the carriage?" I said, "Yes." She said, "I am the lady." I said to my husband, 'I want the man who was so kind to me in my trouble to bury my mother.'" The key of kindness will work.

2. Jesus used the key of love to reach people, to reach the children. Love begets love. How the children loved him. I agree with the hymn writer who wrote "I wish that his hands had been placed on my head, that his arms had been thrown around me and that I might have seen the kind look when he said, Let the little ones come unto me."

3. One of the best keys for prying open the heart's door is prayer. I was holding a meeting in the eastern part of Virginia some years ago and there was a wayward son in the community who had godly parents. All seemed interested in his salvation and were praying for him, but they could not get him to attend the meeting. At the last service, after I started to preach, I noticed a young man come in and sat on the back seat. We sang an invitation hymn and several had come forward' when I turned to the choir and said "Let's sing 'Softly and Tenderly, Jesus Is Calling'," and on the second stanza that young man stepped out and came forward as the audience broke out in tears. That father and mother came to the front and put their arms around him. From this service we were going down to the creek for the Baptizing and the father said, "Son, we are so happy you have come but we wish you had come sooner so we could have brought your change of clothes and let you be baptized with the rest." The old mother said, "Papa, I have his clothes in the back of the car. I didn't sleep a wink last night but I prayed all night and about light this morning I felt sure he was going to come and I got his clothes and put them in the car." Then she said, "His favorite hymn is 'Softly and Tenderly, Jesus Is Calling' and when you called for that (while I had not seen him in church), I knew that God was working."

Let us pray that God may open the hearts of many and come in.

28

How Daniel Became President

He was a young man in a great and wicked city far from home. Few people had more obstacles across their path, and still fewer rose as high as Daniel did. When he was about twenty years of age, he and three of his friends were taken captive from Jerusalem to pagan Babylon. There, faced with all kinds of problems, Daniel became president. There was a pod of five P's that enabled him to overcome and rise in power and influence. We want to look at these five principles and build them into our lives that we too may rise in power and service.

1. The first was a fixed purpose. Daniel purposed in his heart that he would not defile himself with the king's diet. Now is the time for you to fix your purpose in life. Character is usually made or ruined before you are thirty. Many people have no purpose or aim in life. Consequently they do not make progress. The Psalmist said, "My heart is fixed. Aim high and then strive for the goal." Someone has said, "Failure is not the sin but low aim." With Emerson, "hitch your wagon to a star."

2. Thoughtful planning was his second life principle. He did not sit and wait for his lucky day but went into action. When the king's servant came with the king's meat and wine, Daniel proposed a substitute of vegetable diet. When the servant hesitated to accept the substitute, Daniel challenged him to give them a ten day test. He was willing to be put on the spot.

Dr. Broadus would say to his class, "Plan to live seventy-five years." If he was teaching today he would say, "Plan to live one hundred years." Where do you want to be ten years from now? That will be largely determined by how well you plan and execute your plans for the future.

3. Daniel made thorough preparations. If you are to become president you want to begin climbing now. Become president of

your class, your club. Make yourself indispensable in your present position. Jesus said, "He that is faithful in the little things, I will make him ruler over many things." Develop the full-rounded life. Jesus increased in wisdom, stature and in favor with God and man. Paul says to young Timothy, "Make full proof of thy ministry."

4. He developed a dogged persistence. He knew how to keep on keeping on. Jesus said of the early Christians, "Ye are my disciples if ye continue in my teachings." Daniel's obstacles seemed to be insurmountable. It was one thing after another. It would have been easy to say, "Well, this is an impossible task." It is not always the brightest boy or girl in school that is going farthest in life. I think sometimes the student who has to really struggle to make the grade gets something that is essential to success in life that the brilliant student who slides along misses.

5. The last principle that put Daniel over was prayer. Three times a day he looked to Jerusalem and prayed. Daniel had a religious background. He must have had a praying mother. We know he grew up under the tutelage of the old prophet Jeremiah. This religious background was his main anchor in those trying years in Babylon. When he and his associates were thrown into the lion's den and were taken out, there was no hurt upon them because they trusted in God.

You may not become president, but if you incorporate Daniel's five principles in his pod of P's you will get further in life than it would be possible to get without them.

29

A Watch

I hold in my hand a watch which I prize highly. My son, Walton, gave me this watch. He purchased it in Switzerland in 1947. It is an excellent time piece and it has a message for you boys and girls tonight.

1. It has an open face. You can look at its face and get its message. I like to see people with an open face. Your face generally reveals what is in you. Let's keep a clean conscience so we will carry an open face.

2. It is made up of many parts that come from various sources. Each part is important to the usefulness of the watch. If one little part is out of place it can paralyze the entire watch. You may feel that you are a small part of God's great Kingdom but in his sight, you are important. Your presence at your post of duty is necessary to full service of your church. Your close cooperation is essential to its efficiency.

3. This watch must be active to be of service. Merely to be called a watch is not enough. Just to have your name on the church roll is not enough. You need to be functioning. Letting your light shine. We have lots of members in our church who are mere spectators. They are not counting on the team.

4. For this watch to serve, it must be wound up regularly. You cannot wind it enough to run a week but it is to be wound daily. You recall the Bible says, "Give us day by day our daily bread." How do we get wound up? That is done through feeding on the word of God. Regular worship through meditation and service.

5. Of course, for this watch to be of value, it must always tell the truth. Let it become careless and incorrect, it would throw me off the schedule and cause me serious trouble.

Boys and girls, for you and me to be of service to God and his church, we must be dependable.

We are told to be faithful in all things.

30

The Ideal Boy

The world has never known but one ideal boy. Let us look at him and see what we can find in his life that will help us. We don't know a great deal about his boyhood, but what we do know is suggestive.

First we know that he was an industrious boy. At the age of twelve, he said, "I must be about my father's business." Others said of him that he was always going about doing good. When he reached manhood he said, "I must work."

Everybody should be busy. Life is too short and sweet to be wasted in idleness.

In the next place, Jesus was an obedient boy. It was said of him that he came to Nazareth and was subject unto his parents. That is, he obeyed them. There is a verse of a hymn that says "Trust and obey for there is no other way to be happy in Jesus, but to trust and obey." Our happiness and usefulness depends upon our obedience to God. As boys and girls we need to learn the principles of obedience. Obey our parents, our teachers, the law of the land and then it will not be hard to learn to obey God.

Jesus was a religious boy. Early in life he had a consciousness of his relation to his Heavenly Father. He said, "I must be in my father's house." He participated in public worship at twelve years of age. As a man he went into the synagogue as was his custom, on the Sabbath Day. His prayer life was unique. One of the most impressive things about him was his reliance on communion with the father.

He was compassionate. When he saw the multitudes he was moved with compassion for they were as sheep without a shepherd. He didn't look on or express sympathetic words only, but did something about their problem. His idea seems to have been to give light in dark places. I imagine after a busy day with suffering humanity, Jesus could shut his eyes and see the blind, deaf, maimed and lost multitude. It was natural for him to weep.

31

Our Changing Bodies

I didn't ask you to bring me an object tonight because I am going to talk about you. You didn't know that your body goes through almost a complete change about every seven years. I don't mean that you live along for seven years then your body makes a complete change, but it is constantly changing and completes the cycle about every seven years. It is best for you to know this for it will help you to make adjustments, as you go along. I think I can best help you understand this by putting a typical sentence in your mouth describing each period. The first seven years you say, "I want mama." Your mama to you is the center of the universe and you look to her for everything. The next period you have enlarged the circle and you have the play instinct. "Mama, don't make me come in now, I want to play." You have the gang spirit. You want to go camping and hiking with the gang. "I don't want to be with them old gals, I want to play ball." The next period you try to hide it but you will cut your eyes across the aisle at school, and throw a spitball over at the girls and after a while you begin to write notes and pitch them over when the teacher turns her back. One day you will write on a piece of paper, "As sure as the vine grows around the stump, I want you for my sugar lump" and you will throw it across to Susie. Then in a few years you will say, "Susie, wilt thou marry me?" and Susie will wilt and you both will stand before the preacher and say "I will." All will be peaches and cream for several years and one morning after trying to eat the burnt biscuit in a fit of anger you will say, "Well, go on back home to your mama, and see if I care." You slam the door and off to work you go as Susie sits down and cries.

This should not happen with married people for they are now one. They are life's partners. What affects one affects both, but the period of adjustment is not always easy. Some marriages fall on the rocks sometimes and go to pieces during this period. If you will be patient time and change will take care of the situation.

Far along in the next period your eyes will grow dim and your step become unsteady and you begin seriously to think about the future. Have we saved enough to care for us in old age. You will say, "Darling, I am growing old" and you will be drawn closer together than ever before, and you will be more dependent upon each other. Yes, these changes are before you and fortunate are the couples that know it and prepare for it along the way.

32

Good and Bad Habits

What is a habit boys and girls? Get six pieces of paper about an inch wide and four inches long. Number them 1 to 6. On No. 1 write profanity, No. 2 coming late, No. 3 leaving church after Sunday school, No. 4 helping in the singing, No. 5 praying daily and No. 6 telling others of Jesus. Roll each in a ball and hand to six children. Ask No. 1 to read his then ask if that is a good or bad habit. Let the group speak out loud. "Bad" Let's get rid of it. He throws it in a trash can. Profanity is a sinful habit and it is a silly habit. It helps no one. It reveals the fact that one is ignorant and does not have a vocabulary to express himself. When our son was about six years old he and Billy were playing in our yard and my son's mother was inside the house and she heard Billy use a profane word. She stepped to the door and told Billy to go home. Each one asked "Why?" "No boy that uses words like that can play with my boy, Billy." "Aw, Mrs. Connelly, that was nothing. You ought to hear my daddy cuss." "Tell your daddy to come to church and he will learn better than to use such words." No. 2, Always late. Is that good or bad? Throw it in the waste basket. When you get big and are late for business engagements you will lose out. It is a sign of weak character. When Theodore Roosevelt was president, he came into church five minutes late one Sunday and he sat on the back seat. As the service closed he went to the front and apologized to the pastor for being late. He said, "I came upon an accident and helped relieve a suffering one." He said, "I don't have the habit of being late. I regret coming to God's house behind time. Please excuse me." No. 3, Leaving before worship, good or bad? Throw it in the trash can. "Seek me and my kingdom first. Forsake not the assembling of yourselves together." There is something about worshiping together. Fellowship is an essential to growth and those who treat it lightly suffer in their character. How would you feel if you prepared a good meal and invited guests and they came and just as you were ready to serve them, they turned and went home? It is mistreating the minister but worse than that it is an insult to God. No. 4, Helping with the singing. Good or bad? Yes, keep it. Put it in your pocket and don't lose it. Some may say, "I can't sing." But you can. Maybe you can't sing like Beverly Shea but if you don't have that kind of voice you can praise God with what you have. The Bible doesn't say let the choirs sing but let the people praise God and you will feel better if you participate in the service. No. 5, Daily prayer, good or bad? Keep it. Maybe this is our greatest need. When Jesus was in the flesh he seemed to think it was. He prayed daily and before all of his decisions. In my first pastorate a little eleven year old girl came forward one Sunday morning professing faith in Christ. I was in her home the following Saturday and she walked up and laid her Bible in my lap and said, "This is the chapter I read last night." I always read a chapter each night and pray and I always pray for you." She helped her pastor preach better by praying for him. "Ere you left your room this morning did you think to pray?" So when life seems dark and dreary don't forget to pray. No. 6, Bringing others to Jesus. Good or Bad? Keep it. This is our chief business, and we have the opportunities every day. I heard the beloved late Dr. Truett relate this experience. He was holding a meeting and urging all to go and bring others. A small girl about a dozen years old came up to him and said, "I am going after Grandpa." "Who is your Grandpa?" "Don't you know him? He is an infidel. He doesn't come to church." "Well, Minnie, you go ahead and I will pray for you." As she approached the house she saw him out in the garden and he looked up and saw her coming and said, "Hello, Minnie, I'm glad to see you." She said, "I don't know whether you are or not. You don't know what I have come for." He said, "I don't care what you came for, Grandpa is always glad to see you." She reached up and caught hold of his long white beard and said, "Grandpa, I love you and I want you to be saved. The preacher down at our church is telling the people how to be saved." Big tears ran out of his eyes down on his beard. He said, "Alright, Minnie, I'll come tonight." That night Dr. Truett said he saw an old man leaning on his cane, come in and sit near the door. As he closed the sermon he said "All who will accept Jesus tonight will come to the front as we sing." The organist had hardly touched the keys when the old man pulled up on his cane and came down the aisle. God can use you the same way if you will tell the message.

33

Two Bibles

The Bible and a mirror. How many Bibles do you see? In a sense, just one but in another sense, two. As you look into the mirror, who do you see? Self, yes, it reveals self. You are able to see yourself. What you look like. There was a man who had his picture taken. The photographer showed him several proofs and asked which one he wanted. He put a magnifying glass over them and shook his head and said he didn't want either. He had no idea he was so ugly.

As you look in the Bible whom do you see? Who is revealed in the Bible? Yes, God. God is revealed as Father who loves and provides for his children. He is revealed as God in Christ who loved us and gave himself for us. He died to take away our sins. Was buried but rose again and is alive now. He assures us that we will rise from the dead to be with him in a better world. He is revealed as the Holy Spirit who dwells in us and comforts us in sorrow, empowers us for service, guides us in our problems and strengthens us in our temptations.

Which of these two Bibles is more important? Yes, the real Bible is more valuable. It helps in this life and points the way to a better life in the world of tomorrow.

Let me ask you another question. Which one do you look in more often? How often do you look in the mirror? Every day, when you comb your hair, when you boys put on your tie; and you girls, when you powder your nose and paint your cheeks. Yet you agree that the real Bible is more important?

Which one do you keep before you most? I hope you look in the real Bible longer at a time. You should study this to learn about our great God and his plan for our lives. This is a sort of road map to show us the way through life and to God's house. We want to know more about it that we may help our friends and neighbors to know and love God too.

34

Fishing

How many of you boys and girls have ever been fishing? All who would like to go raise your hands. I like to fish too. It is one of the most popular sports with lots of people. Fishing is likewise a most serious business. Jesus said "Come ye after me and I will make you to become fishers of men." Had he been talking to you he would no doubt have said, "fishers of boys and girls." There is a similarity of fishing for boys and girls to fishing for fish. I lived for six years down on the coast where fishing is a big business. I noticed there was one thing that all fishermen did. They fished where the fish were. They didn't sit around in their homes and yards and wait for the fish to come there to be caught. Had they done that, they never would have caught fish.

Where are the lost people that we want to catch? Not many are in the services. We have got to go out to their homes, places of business and schools, etc. to find them. Did not Jesus say, "Go out in the highways and hedges and compel them to come in"? Andrew findeth Simon, Jesus findeth Philip. They widely searched for lost people in the early church.

2. You need to know the fish, know where they stay, what their habits are, what kind of food they eat. We need to know these boys and girls, what they do and what their habits and hobbies are. Therefore, we want to fellowship with them and let them know that we love them and want them saved.

3. To catch fish we have to stay in the background. If the fish sees the fisherman they likely won't bite the hook. Our task is to let our prospects see, not us, but Jesus. We must constantly remind them of him.

I heard a busy pastor say that he was sitting in his study preparing a sermon and he saw a little black-eyed boy peeping in the door. He said, "Come in son. What can I do for you?" He walked in and said, "Dr. Fulks, our mother died last night and we want you to bury her, we hope you won't turn us down." The pastor put his arms around the little fellow and said, "Of course I'll not turn you down." He put on his hat and said, "Take me down to your home." They walked in and found the father and the rest of the family and he comforted them as best he could and went back the next day and held the service. On the following day he was back in his study at work and saw the same little boy looking in the door. "Come in" said the pastor, "what can I do for you today?" Walking in the little boy said, "Dr. Fulks, I have just come to say you remind us so much of Jesus." At first the preacher said it sounded like blasphemy, that he reminded them of Jesus. Upon second thought he said "What am I here for but to remind people of Jesus. Isn't that your task and mine?"

4. We want to be sure we have the right bait when we go fishing. People need and want the Scripture. God has promised to bless it. Let's have it in our hearts, heads and hands and know when and how to use it to fit the particular case with which case we are dealing.

35

Steps in the Christian Life

I often use this as a special message to the boys, girls and young people during a series of meetings.

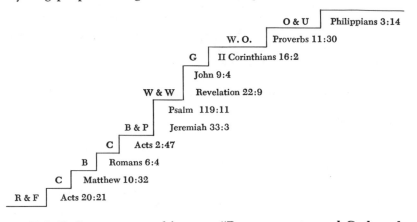

O & U	Philippians 3:14
W. O.	Proverbs 11:30
G	II Corinthians 16:2
	John 9:4
W & W	Revelation 22:9
	Psalm 119:11
B & P	Jeremiah 33:3
C	Acts 2:47
B	Romans 6:4
C	Matthew 10:32
R & F	Acts 20:21

R & F—Let us repeat this verse. "Repentance toward God, and faith toward our Lord Jesus Christ." What do you think that R and F stand for, boys and girls? Repentance and faith. What is repentance? It is turning around—about face. Let us suppose there was no roof on this building and the sun is in the west. As I face the sun, my shadow would be at my back. If I turn around I face my shadow and the sun is at my back. Repentance means turning away from sin and turning to Jesus. What is faith? I heard the late William E. Hatcher explain faith this way. He said that as a boy attending a revival meeting near his home, "I was walking to church one night by myself and soon my uncle joined me from a side road and we were talking as we walked. My uncle said, 'William, have you become a Christian?' I replied that I had not. My uncle asked me 'Why not accept Christ and become a Christian, tonight?' I told him that I didn't understand it. He pointed to a huge oak tree and said, 'William, you see that big limb on that oak tree? Let's suppose that you were up on the limb of that tree, and that I walked up under it and told you to turn loose and jump, that I would catch you. Would you jump?' I told him that I would not jump. He then said, 'Well, William, suppose that Jesus would walk up under this tree and told you to jump and he would catch you, would you jump?' I replied, 'Yes, I would if Jesus said so.' My uncle said, 'Well, William, that is faith. That is acting on the promises of Jesus. If you would yield your life to him, tonight, he will save you.' At that service I accepted Christ and became a Christian."

What is that Letter C for? Let us repeat this verse. "Whosoever confesses me before men, him will I confess before my father in heaven." Yes, it is confess. Jesus wants us to confess publicly. Something happens to us when we definitely confess our faith in him, and he wants to use us in his service, therefore, he wants us to take our stand publicly for him.

What is that letter B for? Let us repeat the verse "Therefore, we are buried with him by baptism into death." Yes, it is baptism. Jesus was baptized and calls upon us to follow his example. Baptism pictures a great spiritual truth that should follow the conversion experience. It reflects what has taken place in our hearts and lives as we accept Christ.

What is that C for? We'll repeat that verse. "The Lord added to the church daily, such as were being saved." Jesus started the church. He said, "I will build my church." He loved the church and gave himself for it. When we become Christians we should dedicate our lives to Christian service and join the body of Christ and seek to serve him through the church.

Now the B & P. Let us repeat these two verses together. B is "Thy word have I hid in my heart that I might not sin against thee." When I accepted Christ, my father gave me a little Testament and asked me to read it daily. It has been my constant companion and a source of strength through the years. This book will keep you from sin and sin will keep you from this book.

The P is for prayer and that verse is "Call unto me, and I will answer thee, and show thee great things." Every Christian should learn to pray. It should be our daily practice. God hears the prayers of his little lambs.

What is the W & W for? To repeat the verse, Jesus said, "I must work the works of him that sent me while it is day. The night cometh when no man can work." We join the church to serve and grow. We cannot afford to be idle. The other W is for worship. That likewise is a means of growth. We honor God as we regularly practice the habits of worship. The Bible says "Forsake not the assembling of yourselves together." Worship helps to make us conscious of God's presence.

What is this G for? Let's look at the verse "Upon the first day of every week let every one of you lay by in store as God has prospered you." Giving is a Christian's grace. It should be a part of our worship. You notice Paul said, "It is upon the first day of the week that we are to bring this offering." That is God's day. The Old Testament told us not to appear before the Lord empty, but bring the offering. You will want to make this your weekly practice.

W. O. means win others. "He that wins souls is wise." When we are saved it is our privilege to witness to others. One is wise who seeks the lost. Jesus can use boys and girls to tell others about him. My son Walton, became a Christian when he was not quite six years of age. He immediately began talking with others about the Saviour. When he was eight years of age, he played a trumpet in the local band. I was holding a meeting in the Healing Springs Church about 25 miles from my home. I asked him if he didn't want to bring his trumpet along and play for the Junior Choir. He was delighted. We arrived at church early and there was only one car on the grounds: the parents and two boys about his age. He played with the boys until the congregation assembled. At the conclusion of the service that night some five or six boys came forward confessing Christ. On our return home he said, "Dad, do you remember the first boy that came up tonight?" I replied, "Yes very well." He said, "I talked to him about becoming a Christian tonight and he told me he wanted to be saved." Jesus can use boys and girls to win others.

O & U means onward and upward. This verse says, "I press toward the mark of the prize of the high calling of God in Christ Jesus." I love the hymn which says, "I'm pressing on the upward way, new heights I'm gaining every day; Still praying as I onward bound, Lord plant my feet on higher ground." It is the Christian's privilege to get on higher ground every day.

Now let us see if you can tell me what each of these initial letters stand for, starting from the bottom step. Thank you, very much. That is fine. Shall we now bow in prayer and I want each Sunday school teacher who will do so, lead audibly in just one sentence of prayer, after which we shall sing the hymn "Just As I Am," and those of you desiring to become Christians will come forward and take the front seats as we sing.

36

The Palm Tree

In Psalm 92:12 we read, "The righteous shall flourish like the palm tree." I had the privilege of spending some time in Cuba in 1920. Among the many things that stand out in my memory are the beautiful palm trees. There are numerous species of palm trees but they are all kin. Those that grow in Florida and Cuba have similarities to those in the Bible lands, referred to in our text. Tonight and tomorrow night I want to draw some lessons from them for you.

1. First, palms grow straight. We drove fifteen miles out from Havanna to the president's home. The lane leading from the highway to the mansion has a row of palm trees on either side. Those trees are so straight that if you stand in line with them you can only see the first tree. The others are directly behind each other. Here is a valuable lesson for us. We should learn to grow straight. There is no place for crooks and curves in our character. We are having difficulties getting along with one of the world powers today, because we cannot trust them.

2. The tree grows very tall. Some as much as eighty feet. The majority around fifty feet. The tree seems to want to get as near heaven as possible. This upward climb, as we shall learn later, is made by overcoming great barriers of weight. The Christian life should be an upward life. The hymn writer was right when he said, "I'm pressing on the upward way, new heights I'm gaining every day." There is always more room at the top. Let's aim high and keep climbing.

3. I noticed that the palm tree has its leaves and fruit up toward the top. It looks as if it would be easy to blow over. But I looked in vain for one that had blown down. Do you know why they stand the winds? It's because they send their roots deep in the soil. If you want to climb high, go deep in your

foundation work. You will need a solid foundation upon which to rest if you are to be a climbing Christian.

4. The palm tree is evergreen. It doesn't waste time at certain seasons of the year. It is never too hot, too cold, too wet or too dry for the palm tree to be about its business. It is thrifty and dependable.

5. The palm tree is useful. Its products are used for 360 different things. The Arabs and Egyptians could live off the palm tree, so the dictionaries tell us. Her fruits, the dates, feed millions. Sap is made into wine and fiber is used for ropes and riggings. Her stems are used for timber and the leaves are made into brushes, mats, bags, couches and baskets. If God can use a tree for so many things, what could he do with us if we learn to obey his law, and grow straight, tall, deep and useful.

6. The palm tree begins to produce early, when it is about eight years old. It is surprising what God can do with a boy or girl who is dedicated to him. The little lad who had only five loaves and two fishes had love for Jesus and was vitally interested in him. Willingly he gave his all to Jesus and Jesus took it and fed the multitudes and enshrined that boy's memory in the sacred halls of fame.

7. The older the palm tree gets the better is its fruit. I believe it is still that way with God's people. We may get too old for certain types of service but never too old to bear fruit. The palm leaves grow to be some twenty five feet in length and curl slightly and gracefully. The winds blow through them and make constant music for the passers-by. We should live in such close touch with God that our lives will cheer and challenge those with whom we come in contact.

8. The palm is an endogen plant. It grows from within. It is weighted down with huge leaves and heavy fruit but it knows no obstacle to growth. Its difficulties are a challenge to its character. As individuals we need to grow from within. It is sad to

see one with a huge physical body but a mental and spiritual dwarf within. In his prayer for the Ephesian Christians as recorded in the third chapter and sixteenth verse, the author prays that "they may be strengthened with might by his spirit in the inner man that Christ may dwell in them." Is not that the need of the individual and the church today? The outward growth is quicker and more glamorous but the inward growth is more lasting and more needed.

The palm leaves were used by the Jews as symbols of peace and victory. In Revelation 7:9 the glorified were described as clothed in white robes and with palms in their hands. You will recall when Jesus was making the triumphal entry into Jerusalem they strewed palm leaves for the animals to walk on. This is a sign of the purpose of his coming to bring peace and give victory.

The hymn writer picked up the strain in the familiar old hymn, "Then palms of victory, crowns of glory, palms of victory I shall wear."

We are following a Christ that knows no defeat. He says, "In the world you will have tribulation but be of good cheer. I have overcome the world." We can flounder and fall and impede the progress of the Kingdom but we cannot defeat it. The church may blunder but remember that Jesus said "the gates of hell shall not prevail against it."

37

The Mission of a Tooth Brush

1. You perhaps had never thought about the tooth brush having a message for you but it does. The Rev. Mr. Tooth brush says one of my duties is to help your appearance. Pretty, clean white teeth will add to the appearance of anyone. And our first appearance is very important. Recently my pastor asked me if I could suggest to him a good leader to train his choirs and I replied, "Yes, I believe I can name the person who will suit you." I told him about her excellent character and attitude, her thorough training and experience and other fine qualities. He then turned to me and asked just one more question: "What about her appearance? I need an attractive personality." A girl in our training school would pray "Lord make me winsome for thy sake."

2. The tooth brush helps to preserve your teeth. By cleaning them daily you prevent cavities from starting. It is not much pleasure to sit back in a dentist chair and have the dentist pull your teeth. This often is not necessary if the teeth are properly cared for.

3. Not only will the brush help preserve your teeth but it will help protect your general health. A brother of mine had been in poor health for months and the doctor thought he had cancer of the stomach and put him in the hospital saying he would not live over two or three months. That was forty-five years ago and he is still living. The doctors in the hospital said his teeth were poisoning his entire body They extracted them and he was soon back at work.

4. For the brush to help it must be used. It is of no value in the holder on the wall. It is like safety belts they will not protect unless they are buckled around you.

These same laws that apply to the tooth brush are applicable to our spiritual life. Christianity blesses us when we apply the Christian principles to our daily lives.

38

A Pair of Scissors

Let's see, boys and girls, what we can learn from this queer looking preacher today.

1. He says, "I cannot produce when I am all crossed up." You have to bring both sides together before he will function. That is a valuable lesson for us to learn early in life. That is true of individuals who have split personalities. They get all crossed up and confused and are unable to get themselves together. There are also families who get crossed up and begin to pull apart and it does not take long for them to go on the rocks. It is a sad fact but churches get crossed and cannot function. When Pentecost came they were all of one accord in one place. Nothing will paralyze a church as quickly as for the members to get cross with each other and begin to pull apart. We church people should set an example to the rest of the world on how to work together. The world has been in serious trouble across the ages, and we have had these horrible wars because we would get cross with each other.

2. For the scissors to function properly they must not only be together but be sharp. We have to grind the blades and keep a good edge on each. If we are to function we too must constantly be sharpened. We sharpen our wits and clarify our minds by studying and learning constantly. That is why we go to school, to Sunday School and church. These drop outs are going to lose out in life because they cannot compete with those who prepared for tomorrow.

3. The scissors have to be guided by a power outside of themselves. A hand must push the blades in the desired direction. Each of us needs guidance from a source above us. Our all wise Heavenly Father has provided us this help. The Bible tells us in the sixteenth chapter of John that when the Holy Spirit comes

He will guide us into all Truth. We cannot function apart from Him. Jesus said apart from Me ye can do nothing. He gives us power for the task and guidance in our decisions. He expects us to bear fruit for Him, but we must have His power and guidance to be fruitful for His Glory.

39

Growth

Boys and girls, we are going to talk about something that concerns each of us.

You see this acorn. This acorn has in it the possibility of becoming a giant tree. It takes time and care, but with the proper treatment it will become a tree. I have several huge oaks in my yard at home. A man recently said to me, "I wouldn't take a thousand dollars for it if I had that tree in my yard." That tree was once a little acorn like this, and it has taken more than fifty years to become what it is today.

Boys and girls, you have in you the possibilities of growth. You have passed out of the acorn stage and have become a bush. I want you to grow into a strong healthy tree. The Bible says Jesus increased in wisdom, and stature and in favor with God and man. He grew physically, mentally, socially and spiritually. That is what we want to do too, isn't it? We want to develop the four square life. We don't want to be one-sided. One time I saw a man about forty years old who was less than three feet tall. He failed to grow physically. He was called a midget. I have seen lots of mental, social and spiritual midgets.

We grow physically by eating the proper food, getting plenty of exercise, fresh air and rest. Now there are laws of growth in the other areas of life just like there are in the physical area. Let's learn these laws and obey them that we may mature into the full rounded out life. We develop our minds by exercising and feeding them; train ourselves to think; concentrate on what we are doing. Let's make our school days count for the most. My old teacher in the Seminary taught me to keep a book on my desk that would require deep thought to understand and to read it some each day.

We grow socially by mingling with people and cultivating their acquaintance and friendship. We don't have to agree with them necessarily, but try to like them and if possible befriend them. Will Rogers said, "I have never met a man I didn't like." We need friends and we win friends by being friendly.

We perhaps have more spiritual midgets than we have physical, mental or social ones. There are laws of growth in this area the same as there are in the other areas of life. We need to cultivate the presence of God. The Psalmist cried, "Cast me not away from thy presence." The first step is to receive Jesus as your personal Saviour and Lord and to acknowledge Him before others. Read His word daily for then we will become better acquainted with Him. Cultivate the acquaintance and friendship of older people who have known Him for years. Have a quiet place to go alone and talk with Him daily. Attend and participate in the public services of your church. Seek to serve others and to lead them to know Him as their Saviour and Lord. There is no better time than now to begin obeying the laws of growth that you may be a strong mature Christian.

40

A Dedicated Heart

What is this card the shape of, boys and girls? "A heart,"; that is right. And we are going to talk about the heart this morning.

We think of the heart as the center of affection and of the will. It is the basis of your whole personality. The Bible says, "As a man thinketh in his heart so is he." "Out of the heart are the issues of life." In Proverbs 23:26 it says, "Give me thine heart." The four little monosyllables carry a vital message to each of us. I want you to decide today what you will do with your heart. Satan wants it and is asking for it too.

1. God has a right to ask for your heart. It belongs to Him for three reasons.

(a) God made our heart and He has never released His claim on it. Satan is an intruder trying to break in and steal it away.

(b) When man willfully fell from God, he went into sin. God bought us back. The Bible says "Ye are not your own, ye are bought with a price." Nor silver nor gold can obtain my redemption nor riches of earth can save my poor soul. The blood of the Cross is my only Salvation.

During the days of slavery, they were selling slaves on the block in New Orleans. They put up a young mother and were auctioneering her off. She was crying as she thought of the separation from her family. A young Christian business man looking on was touched as he thought of this mother being sold away from her home and loved ones. So he bought her and told her that he bought her to set her free and go live with her people. At first she was frightened and cried louder. But she saw him pay the money and realized what he had done. She got down on her knees and said, "I don't want to go home. I

want to go to your home and live with you and be your servant."
If we could really take in what God has done for us we would
each want to serve Him the rest of our lives.

(c) Another reason God has a claim to our heart is because
God has adopted us into His Family. We are heirs of God and
joint heirs with Christ. Yes, we belong to Him.

2. There is no substitute for this gift. No amount of money or
property given to His cause will satisfy Him. He says, "I seek
not yours but you." A wicked kidnapper stole a baby from the
arms of its mother. No gift of money or no other baby as a gift
would satisfy the mother. She wanted her baby back. When
Paul was writing of the church in Macedonia he said, "First
they gave themselves to the Lord."

3. Nothing else will satisfy us. We are made by God for Him,
and as Augustine said, we will find no rest until we rest in
Him. "As the hart panteth after the water brooks, so panteth
my soul after Thee, O God." When our four year old son was
having his tonsils removed they would not let his mother in the
recovery room. He was restless and crying for her but as soon
as she touched him and said, "Mother is here," he relaxed and
went to sleep. That satisfied him.

4. This means a wholehearted surrender, full and complete.
God wants our all dedicated to Him. Someone was commending
General Booth, founder of the Salvation Army, for his great con-
tribution and asked how he accomplished so much. He said,
"God has all there is of me."

As a boy I learned a little poem that has been a blessing to
me and I pass it on to you.

> Oh the bitter pain and sorrow that a time could ever be
> When I proudly said to Jesus all for self and none for Thee
> Day by day His tender mercies healing helping full and free
> Brought me lower while I whispered less for self and more
>   for Thee.

Higher than the highest heavens
Deeper than the deepest sea
Lord Thy love at last has conquered
None for self but all for Thee.

During the Civil War, when the Army of Northern Virginia was playing an important part in the struggle, General Lee said to one of his scouts, "Tell General Jackson the next time he is up this way to call and see me about a matter of no great importance." The next morning as General Lee was preparing for breakfast a soldier told him that General Jackson was outside to see him. He walked out and said, "General Jackson, I didn't want you to ride this eight miles through the snow and zero temperature to see me. That is why I said, 'see me about a matter not too important.'" General Jackson replied, "The slightest wish of General Lee is to me a supreme command." That is the loyalty and devotion that God deserves and wants from us.

5. God says, "Give me your heart like it is, and I will make it what it should be and give it back to you. The mother earth asks for a tiny seed; it gives back a strong plant. It asks for an ugly bulb; it gives back a beautiful lily. God asked for the heart of Saul, the persecutor; He gave back Paul the great preacher. Won't you give Him your heart today, and let Him make of you what He wants you to be.

41

Come—Go

Boys and girls, what are these two words on this card? "COME, GO." These two words shine out upon the pages of the Old and New Testament. The Prophet of old said, "Come let us reason together, saith the Lord." "Ho everyone that thirsteth, Come." Jesus says in the New Testament, "Come unto me all ye that labor and are heavy laden"; "Follow Me."

Jesus invites us to come to Him with our burdens and He will give us rest. Come to Him with our problems and He will help us solve them. Come to Him and He will give us power for His service.

Someone said that directly and indirectly we have 642 invitations in the Bible to come to the Divine Source for help. We are invited to *come* to be prepared to *Go*. The book of Revelation speaks of coming out and coming up. We have to come out of sin before we can come up to salvation. We are to come to Jesus and be cleansed and empowered to go. It would be interesting to take a concordance and see how many times we are told to go. "Go ye into all the world." "Go out into the highways and hedges." "Go . . . to the lost sheep."

Jesus set the example. He was always going about doing good. He sent others. First the Twelve, then the Seventy, then the whole church—all were to go and tell. This includes the boys and girls who have already come to Him and have been saved. Many times Jesus used the boys and girls, and I am sure He is here today looking for boys and girls who are willing to be used.

There was an unsaved father playing with his little girl one day. And she said "Daddy, do you have your soul insured?" He said, "Jane, why did you ask me that question?" She replied,

"Uncle Jim told me you had your car insured, your house insured, and your life insured. I was just wondering if you had your soul insured. That is more important than all the rest. That was the center shot that brought that father to Jesus. That little girl was used of God to bring her father in. I am wondering if there are not unsaved fathers, mothers, brothers, sisters and friends of you Christian boys and girls that you might bring to Jesus. Suppose you tell Jesus that you love Him and want to see others brought to Him and ask Him to help you go out and find them bring them to Him.

I read of a little cripple boy who lived in London. He was confined to his bed. He could not rush and play like other boys and girls of his age. But he loved Jesus and wanted others to love and serve Him. So he asked his mother to buy him a new Bible and a tablet. And he would lie on his bed beside the window and write verses of Scripture like "Prepare to meet thy God." "Look unto me and be saved." "Him that cometh unto me I will in no wise cast out." And he would throw them out of the window down on the side walk. People would pick them up and read them and would begin thinking about becoming Christians. Then they asked who was throwing them out the window, and when they learned it was the little cripple boy they would go up to his room and he would tell them about Jesus and lead them to trust Him. They would tell others and they would come. This went on until there were streams of people daily coming to talk with him. When he died it was said that doubtless he had won more souls to Christ than any other person in London—unless it was Charles H. Spurgeon.

Jesus can use you too to help others know Him. Why not tell others of Him?

44

A Little Boy and His White Rabbit

Early in my ministry I accepted a church that was in a deplorable condition. The building was inadequate and the section of the city was not promising. Several of my close friends advised against my accepting the work. I drove over the area and talked with some of the people and I felt impressed that there was a real need and I should go. The work was not easy but when it finally got started it was an inspiration to work with those people.

I have given this background to tell you how a little boy about four or five years of age was used to help me. We desperately needed some Sunday school rooms. The leaders were reluctant to go in debt. So we set a time when we would try to raise, in cash and pledges, most of the money necessary to build. Then I presented the need, showed the proposed plans and was asking the people to stand and tell what they would give. At first a good many substantial gifts for that group were called out; but then the service bogged down. It was about to become embarrassing when this little four year old boy stood up in a chair and with a loud, clear voice said, "Mr. Connelly, I got a white rabbit I'll give you." It electrified the group. One man got up and said, "If that little fellow will give up his pet that I happen to know he loves dearly, I can make a sacrifie too." And he called out a liberal amount and one after another responded liberally and cheerfully and enough was raised to start the building and when it was completed the cash was in hand to pay the bill.

Some months after that this same little boy came up the street by himself to Sunday school. As he approached the building he stopped and burst out crying. I ran to him thinking a wasp had stung him. I asked, "Seldon, what is the matter?" Looking up through his tears he said, "Me forget me envelope." I said,

"Don't cry. I will watch you across the street and you can run home and get it." In a few minutes he returned with a radiant smile holding up his envelope saying, "I got it now."

About the time I started in the active ministry I read an article written by Russell H. Conwell about how a little boy's gift of a few cents helped him to build a church in a needy section. This was a community of poor people and for some time they had talked about building a new church and they set a certain Sunday to raise funds for the new building. They asked Dr. Conwell to come and preach and help raise the necessary funds. There was a crippled boy in the section who had saved a few pennies. I don't recall the exact amount, but it was less than a dollar's worth and it was all he had. The boy asked his mother to mail it to Dr. Conwell the week preceding the time for the offering and Dr. Conwell took those pennies into the pulpit with him and told the story of the little boy and how he had given his all. The congregation was tremendously moved and enough money was raised that day to assure the building. We can count on the boys and girls, and the church makes a big mistake if they do not use them.

42

A Telephone

You have heard it said many times in a joking way, that three of the fast ways to spread the news are telegraph, telephone and tell a woman. If the men were as loyal to Jesus and as faithful in giving out his message as the women are, we would make greater progress in the kingdom. They were the last to leave the cross and the first to reach the empty tomb. Across the years they have been a challenge to the Christian forces. Now we can add two other means of rapid communications, the radio and television. We have not learned to get the maximum benefit from the modern inventions. I often wonder what Paul would do if he were living today. Let's see if we can learn some lessons in communication from the telephone.

1. The telephone must be connected with the person to whom you desire to speak. This illustrates the Bible teaching of prayer. Before you can get a message through you must be connected with God. In II Chronicles 7:14 we read, "If my people, which are called by my name, shall humble themselves, and pray, and seek my face, and turn from their wicked ways; then will I hear from heaven, and will forgive their sin, and will heal their land." The first condition is that we must be God's people, "my people." You must be in touch with Him through faith in Christ. You must be a member of his family, "called by my name." Dare to be called His own child! Get rid of all static. This is done through humility and prayer and seeking his face and turning from all evil. Then we can hear from Heaven and He says He will forgive our sins and heal our land.

2. The equipment has to be kept in repair. The telephone company keeps a large force of men regularly for this purpose. Storms and falling trees may break the line and cut off com-

munications. There are evil forces within us and around us that will put us out of repair. This demands constant care on our part. The Bible says, "Let him that thinketh he stands take heed lest he fall." The best of us can get out of repair and full of static.

3. The telephone gives and takes the message. Prayer is talking to God and it is also listening to God. We are told to wait on the Lord. Often we rush into God's presence with our problems and burdens telling Him about them and asking for help and then not waiting for His message to us. One of the problems with the phone is the line is often busy. Now we have a direct access to God but so often we get too busy to pray. God's end of the line is never too busy to hear us. The problem is at our end. We get in a big hurry and live in so much noise and confusion that we don't take time to pray. The hymn writer raises the question:

> Ere you left your room this morning
> Did you think to pray?
> So when life seems dark and dreary,
> Don't forget to pray.

43

The Meaning of the Cross

I recently attended the funeral service of a near relative in another city. One of the officiating ministers told about a picture of the cross that hung on the wall of the sick lady's room. It was given to her by the head nurse who was a devoted Christian. My sick relative who lay in her hospital bed interpreted that picture to all the nurses and everyone else who entered the room.

She talked about three symbols. The dark background surrounding the cross pictured her suffering and agony in the human body and the sin of which each of us is guilty. The light on the cross symbolized Jesus hanging there as the light of the world, inviting all in the darkness to come to the light and receive forgiveness. The evergreen at the foot of the cross symbolized eternity. It is an everlasting salvation that was purchased on the cross.

The cross to me means that man is guilty of sin for which only death could atone. Without the shedding of blood there is no remission of sin. The Cross reveals God's hatred of sin and his unchanging love for sinners.

I love the hymn that says,
 "Oh the love that drew Salvation's plans,
 Oh the Grace that brought it down to man.
 Oh the mighty gulf that God did span at Calvary."

It reveals the fact that this was the only way for man to be saved.

In the garden Jesus prayed, "Father, if it be possible let this cup pass from me, nevertheless not my will but thine be done." Since God is not willing that any should perish but all come to repentance, it was his will that Jesus die the cruel death on the cross. It means the vilest of sinners may come to Jesus and receive forgiveness. The best will have to come by way of the cross to be saved. And the worst sinners may come by the same way and be saved. My sins and your sins nailed him to the cross. I have trusted him as my Saviour and Lord. Have you accepted him? If not won't you accept Him while we sing

> "I am coming to the Cross,
> I am poor and weak and blind,
> I am counting all but loss.
> I shall full Salvation find."

45

Types of Church Members

In the parable of the sower Jesus tells us about the good and bad seeds. This reminds me of the kind of church members we have. There are good and bad types. We may illustrate this by some little creatures that are common about our home. Lets look at some of the bad types first.

1. *There is the Snail Type.* One thing we know about the snail; it moves slowly. There are many church members who are wedded to the status quo. They are opposed to change. If they move at all, it is at a snail's pace.

2. *Then we have the Grasshopper Type.* The chief characteristics of the grasshopper are hopping and eating. He will light on a plant and eat until satisfied and hop to another one and on he goes all day. There are members who will go to church for a little while then fall out and quit and join another church.

3. *There is the Chamelon Type.* This little creature is sometimes called a tree frog. He will climb a tree and he has a way of changing the color of his skin to match the tree he is on. He conforms to his surroundings. When he is in Rome he does as Rome does. Paul says we are not to conform to the world's standard but we are to transform ourselves and surroundings to the Christian standard.

4. *There is the Cuckoo Type.* The cuckoo is a bird that is too lazy to build his own nest but will find another bird's nest and will run the owner off and take over the nest for his family. That is what Paul meant when he said we are not to build on another man's foundation. This is a most selfish spirit. Jesus said He came not to be ministered unto but to minister. Some try to make their light look brighter by putting their neighbor's light out. That is the opposite of Christianity.

5. *Lastly we find the Termite Type.* The termite makes no contribution to society but he is wholly destructive. Some people can only destroy. They work in a church like a termite in a house. The termite won't come out in the light but stays in the dark and works from within. I once heard John R. Sampey present George Truett to an audience. He said Dr. Truett is all plus. The termite type is all minus.

Now that we have talked about the bad type church member let's also look at some of the good types.

1. *I think of the Mocking Bird Type.* They sing their way through life. It is hard to be blue and despondent among the mocking birds. They are always dispensing cheer and happiness. I remember George W. McDaniel speaking before the student body of the University of Richmond saying, "Learn to sing while you work." It helps you stay relaxed and you will live longer and produce better if you stay relaxed. I have just returned from the hospital visiting an attractive lady forty-three years of age who is not likely to live long because her nervous, tense nature has adversely affected her health and has cut off her productive years in the prime of life.

2. *There is the Dove Type of member.* This is a gently, harmless bird that quietly goes about its task interfering with no one. You often hear the remark, "harmless as a dove." We need more members like this. The Bible says "Be ye kind one to another tender hearted forgiving one another." One of the chief problems before the world today is how to bring peace to the world and maintain it. Peace depends upon inward conditions of life. Let us strive to emulate the qualities of the dove and be peacemakers in our generation.

3. *There is the Humming Bird Type.* Unlike the vulture who soars around in the air looking for decayed spots to light on, the little humming bird flies around looking for the most beautiful spots to light on and feed. He visits the lily, the rose

and the sweet flower and feeds upon them. That is the nature of that bird. You can pretty well judge a person by the things he seeks. Let us learn to look for the good and emphasize that. Someone has said that there is good in every life. If we will look for it we will find. You will help people by emphasizing these features. Now these good qualities can be cultivated. While we are boys and girls lets learn to develop them as we grow.

46

Living above the Snakeline

(I frequently use this as a special youth message on Saturday night in revivals.)

If we are going to preach tonight we should have a text and I am announcing that I will preach from it, as we preachers sometimes do, Matthew 14:23, "Jesus went up into a mountain."

Jesus must have loved the mountains. They figure prominently in his ministry. He went up into the mountains to pray, to teach, be transfigured and to ascend back to his father. I wish someone would write a book on Jesus and the mountains. How many of you have seen a mountain? When I was a boy I heard the story of a mountain that had lots of snakes in it. Black snakes, green snakes, striped snakes, brown snakes, long snakes, short snakes, all kinds of snakes. I had a friend who had made an extensive study of snakes who said there were only three kinds of snakes in this country that were poisonous. The rattler, the copperhead and the water moccasin, but whether they are dangerous or not, I am afraid of them. I don't want them around me.

When I was a small boy growing up on a farm down in Campbell County, Virginia, they gave me a basket and told me to go to the hen house and gather up the eggs. They said if there was an old hen on the nest to scare her off and get the eggs. I found two eggs in the first nest, several in each of the other nests, until I got to the last nest. It was rather dark and I thought a black hen was on the nest so I started to reach in and push her off when a huge coiled black snake jumped at me. In a few seconds I was back at the house yelling "snake, snake." We had scrambled eggs for the next meal.

Now the interesting thing about that mountain was that after you go up a certain altitude, there are no snakes up there.

There are rocks, trees, water and other growth but no snakes. Now I want to ask you a question. "Where would you rather live, above or below the snakeline?" Yes, and I would too. I want to get as far from danger as possible. I am going to draw a line across this board and call it the snakeline and I want to show you some things above and below it and let you decide on which side you would rather live.

Sin is below the snakeline. I am more afraid of sin than I am of a snake. The snake may kill my body but he cannot reach my soul. But sin can condemn my soul. There are two things about sin I want you to remember.

1. Deceitful—We have sin within and do not realize it. The sinner does not realize the danger in which he is living. If he did, he would repent and turn to Jesus. I knew a girl one time who had the habit of walking in her sleep. One warm night when the windows were all up, the father heard the tin over his front porch popping. He thought about the habit of his daughter walking in her sleep, so he rushed into her room and jumped through the window and seized her as she was about to step off the roof. That would have landed her on the hard pavement below. It could have killed her, but she was asleep to her danger. Many are spiritually asleep tonight to their danger. They don't realize it.

2. Grows—I want you to remember that sin grows. James 1:15 said, "When lust conceives, it brings forth sin and when sin is full grown, it brings death."

Did you ever bite into an apple and find a worm inside? The outside was solid so how did that worm get in there? Yes, when it was only a tiny bud an insect planted an egg and the apple grew over it and it hatched and began to eat the very heart out of that apple. Now the Bible says all have sinned. The soul that sins shall die. How are we going to get rid of sin? We shall take that up in a few mintes, but I want to think about what is above that snakeline to live for.

Schools—What about our schools? Are they above or below. Let's write that word down on the board. How many of you go to school? When we go to school, we are preparing ourselves for a bigger and finer life. So we want all of our boys and girls to study and learn to make good in life.

Sunday School—Above or below? Let's write that word down on the board. How many of you go to Sunday school? That is fine. Here we learn about God who made us and his plan for our lives. As we study his word, we learn of that plan and seek to fit ourselves into it.

Church—What about the church, above or below? Yes, above. Let's write that word on the board. Jesus said "I will build my church." His churches are for the saved people. Those who have accepted him as their Saviour and Lord and dedicated themselves to love and follow him in all of life's relations. We should not join the church until we first forsake our sins and trust him to forgive us and keep us. Then we join the church to grow more like him and serve him daily.

We were saying a few minutes ago that all of us have sinned and come short of his glory and we asked what can we do about it. With this piece of red chalk I want to draw a picture of the cross right in the middle of the snakeline. Why am I using red chalk, boys and girls? That is right. It reminds us of his blood. In 1 John 1:7 it says the blood of Jesus Christ, his Son, is cleansing us from all sin. We go from a life of sin up over the snakeline under the shadow of the cross. The best time to start the Christian life is while we are boys and girls. I want you to think about putting your trust in Jesus and living above the snakeline. Before we go I want to tell you a story.

There was a little girl who had been sick for a long time and now the grass was green, the flowers were beginning to grow and the birds were beginning to sing. Her mother moved her bed over near the window where she could see out and enjoy the new spring life. She becames interested in a little bird that was building her nest near the ground in the tree. Helen said "Little bird, you had better build your nest up higher." But the little bird kept bringing the roots and straw and weaved them into her house. After awhile there were four little blue eggs in it and then there were four little birdies. Helen delighted in watching the mother bird bring in a worm and drop it into a hungry mouth as each would throw wide open his bill for his breakfast. One morning Helen slept a little late and waking up and seeing the bright sunshine, she turned over to look at her birdies. But to her horror, she saw the nest turned upside down and the little birdies gone. On old snake had crawled up in the night and swallowed all of them. And the old mother bird was hopping from limb to limb weeping as if her heart would break. Then Helen said, "Ah little bird, I told you to build your house up higher." Let us bow in prayer as we ask God to help each of us build his life up high, even on the solid rock, Christ Jesus.

PRAYER: Dear Jesus we pray that we may tonight make up our minds to let thee into our hearts and build our lives upon thee that we may live above the snakeline.

Now for our benediction, I want the pastor to come and stand here at the front, and then I want all the boys and girls to come and stand around him and then all of their fathers and mothers come and stand around them as we sing two verses of "Oh, How I Love Jesus," after which the pastor will lead the closing prayer asking God to prepare us for the closing services of our series tomorrow.

47

The Art of Putting a Church to Work

There are too few Christians who realize the importance of having a Spirit-filled, united, active church, especially for our boys and girls. We do not develop character and get preachers and missionaries out of cold, dead, fussing churches. The spiritual lives of children and young people can be seriously and permanently impaired by the unchristian, indifferent churches to which they go. I am, therefore, impressed to close this series with a message on "The Art of Putting a Church to Work." Let me draw you a picture of the average church today.

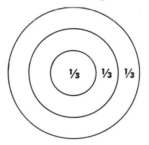

That inner one-third is a group of active, giving, worshiping members. They are up and out for the Lord. The second group are in and out. They attend when it's real convenient. They give when they come, and respond fairly well when you personally call on them. The outer third are down and out. They merely have their names on the church roll and that is the only evidence they have that they are Christians. You might shoot all of them and it would not affect your church or Sunday school attendance, your income, or any other part of the church life, in the least. You take a church of 1800 members and you would have approximately 600 in each group. The Communists say, "We are going to lick you because there is only a small working group of Christians and all of us are working." The sad part about our plight is that many are accepting this as all right. They do not expect or try to improve it.

A young minister said to Mr. Spurgeon, "Why is it that every time you preach, somebody is saved? I preach the same gospel but often there is no response." Mr. Spurgeon said, "You don't expect someone to be saved every time you preach, do you?" "Oh, no" he said. "But" said Mr. Spurgeon, "I expect it every time I preach."

Let's change this attitude in our churches. All that you do preparing for a soul-winning campaign to reach lost people in the community, do within your church to reach the outer circles.

1. Know who and where they are.

2. Love and pray for them.

3. Promote a cultivating campaign, assign certain families in the outer circles to those in the inner circle.

4. Assign responsibility to all you can that they may feel a part of the church.

5. Keep a project or projects before the church. It could be a mission point where you use them.

6. Get them in the church organizations.

7. Help them realize that they should come to the services to worship and serve and not to be served. While their presence helps the cause of Christ their absence hurts it.

Have you ever listed the different things that each of you can do for your church? Attend the services, pray, sing, give, invite others, welcome visitors, witness to the lost. Live the Christ life before the community. A little girl in a slum area caught Helen Gould by the hand one day and looked up in her face and said, "Say Lady, are you Jesus' wife?" Has anyone ever asked if you were related to Jesus?

8. When you hold revival services plan to have your leaders meet before and after the regular worship services and enlist them in enlisting others. It is an excellent time to put over your financial program.

When I had Dr. Burroughs with me at Orcutt Avenue Church, he preached a strong stewardship sermon one Sunday morning. He made the remark that a revival that could not stand some stewardship doctrine wasn't much of a revival. In a meeting at Waverly Church, Roanoke, Virginia, I preached one Sunday morning on our partnership with God and I stressed tithing strongly. There were ten professions of faith. We need to teach people the Christian principles of stewardship instead of criticizing them for not practicing it.

9. Let the pastor preach on the 100 per cent church. Make a list of each family arranged alphabetically with addresses and phone numbers and give each family a copy. Then each organization can easily call their members and also call their prospects. Appoint a telephone committee and assign each about a dozen homes. On many occasions, such as revival and any special occasion, you can in a few minutes get in touch with every family. Stress the importance of all those participating. When I came to Melrose church in 1923, I asked the financial secretary how many regular givers they had. He said, "About 250." They were reporting 1400 members. I said "What about the other 1150?" He said, "Some of them give spasmodically." I asked him, "How often do they have a giving spasm?" He replied "Not often enough." We set out to enlist every resident member and in a year's time there were more than 1100 regular givers and in a few years the income of the church tripled. I have had practically the same experience at several other places. It can be done.

10. Let me share with you my experience with the first church I tried to pastor. Near the close of my freshman year in Rich-

mond College I accepted a church about sixty miles from Richmond. They had about 200 members. When I returned to the church on my second trip, for the Saturday afternoon church meeting which was held once a month, three of the brethren with sad faces walked out to the car and said, "Brother Connelly, our church is ruined." I asked, "What is the matter?" They replied, "Brother X is dead. We buried him last Thursday. He died suddenly. We started to send for you but we knew you were busy in school so we got a neighbor pastor to bury him. The church is bound to go down and it will hurt your ministry to have your first church go down with you. We have talked about it and it certainly worries us." I asked, "Why does the church have to go down?" They said, "You see, we all depended upon Brother X. He was such a good man. He was our Sunday school superintendent, teacher of adult class, and led the singing. He was clerk and treasurer, the only member that leads in prayer. He held every position in the church except president of Womans Missionary Society. The only reason he didn't have that was because they didn't ask him." They were right. The church was dead and buried. It was a willing church. One member willing to do all the work and they were willing for him to do it. "Well," I said, "we have to distribute this work out among others." They said, "We thought so, and we have been thinking and talking about it. Ennis there, said he would try to be superintendent of Sunday school. Jim said he would be treasurer. I'll try to teach the Bible class." I said, "Alright, we will go in and have our business meeting and one of you make a motion that the pastor appoint a nominating committee and I will put you three men and two women on it, and we will meet after church and work out a report for the service tomorrow." If there was ever a desert that bloomed as a rose, that spiritual desert did. College was out in about a month and I located on the field.

There was a horseshoe gallery in the building and it had not been used for years but soon it was full of worshipers. Then they called me young Spurgeon, but it didn't swell my head for I knew if you had only a phonograph in the pulpit with the church members working like they were, the people would fill the church. It is easy to get a group of capable leaders in a church and depend on them carrying on the work and have a great mass and unenlisted people looking on.

It should be our concern to provide for the development of the entire church family. If the church is too large to use all of them, start another church. Soon each church will be doing as much as the one was doing.